GET THAT COURSE ONLINE

The step-by-step guide for experts who want to increase their impact and income

GINETTE TESSIER

Get That Course Online: the step-by-step guide for experts who want to increase their impact and income

Cover design, illustration, typesetting and all graphical elements: Phil Tessier
Author photo © Ginette Tessier

First edition published by Acuitas CTD Ltd, Bournemouth, UK, 2023

ISBN: 978-1-7391409-0-8 (Paperback)
ISBN: 978-1-7391409-1-5 (eBook)

The Get That Gang:
Get That Brand Online
Get That Course Online
Get That Funnel Online
Get That Mindset Online
Get That Video Online
Get That Website Online

CONTENTS

FOLLOW THE RULES UNTIL YOU KNOW ENOUGH TO BREAK THEM

A huge reason for wannabe creators never finishing their online course is the overwhelm that comes from getting too many conflicting sources of advice.

What you'll find in this book is enough information to get that first (or next) course created and selling.

Once you have done that, you will be ready to flex, bend and even break the 'rules' I show you, to suit what you want to achieve.

For every piece of guidance I give you, you will likely find a dozen or more 'experts' claiming that something different is better. Maybe it is.

What I am about to show you is best practice — which is to say it works very well for most people, most of the time. It is also just a starting point — a way to get one done.

Keep that as your highest focus. Because until you have experienced my entire process from start to finish, you won't know enough to know what's going to work for you. So, let's get started and Get That Course Online!

INTRODUCTION

A short (ish) note from your author

My very first online course was a complete disaster. Actually, that's not strictly true. The training content was solid, but everything else... well, let's just say it wasn't going to win any awards.

In fact, when I put my first online course together, the only thing I knew was how to design a training course. As it turned out, I didn't know how to do that either — at least not for pre-recorded online delivery.

I can say with extreme confidence that I have committed every single mistake it's possible to make with online training. Some of them twice. *<embarrassed cough>*

Part of the reason for this was my own stubbornness in wanting to learn how to create online courses myself — after all I was a trainer, so it couldn't be that hard, could it? Part of it was that there just wasn't the help available for what I wanted.

I could find plenty of ways to learn how to market my course. Lots of ways to learn how to make money out of it. This was in the early days of online course creation just starting to become easily available to individuals. Even though this was only around the middle of the 2010s, that's a lifetime for how the industry's developed.

What I couldn't find was anyone talking about how to create courses that did what they were supposed to — deliver effective training. No-one was talking about best practice. Apart from a relatively few instructional designers (who'd had eLearning to themselves for a decade or so) no-one was talking about how to make the whole experience of taking an online course an effective one.

I went about trying to gather as much data as I could about what made a great online course. It helped that my former corporate role had been as a Head of Insight and Performance — so gathering and interpreting information was a natural path.

It took about six months to research and collate and learn and try different things before I was able to compile a best practice checklist for creating an effective and engaging online course. That checklist is still just as relevant today. Find out how to get your copy at the end of this Introduction.

There's still a lot of noise out there from people who think selling online courses about selling online courses is both 'new', 'easy' and a quick way to a fast buck. It's the reason why, for the longest time, I resisted having any sales slant to my training.

I thought that teaching how to sell online courses wasn't something I could or wanted to do — I wasn't a sales trainer after all. And I wasn't selling that many courses myself at that point. I really hated the idea of being one of the sleazy-self-appointed sales gurus I was seeing all the time in social media.

Around this time too, I made my first big personal development purchase. The business was going well enough to afford it and I really needed help to understand the bits of the course creation process that I was missing. I was getting plenty of traction with my free courses but getting people onto the paid ones was more of a struggle.

Once I had completed that development (I created a podcast, a couple of course launches and a virtual summit along the way), I went back to my creation process and re-wrote the entire thing — to take selling into account from the very beginning. And it worked like a charm. Suddenly I knew where I'd gone wrong and where I could help others avoid the same mistakes I'd made.

Now I was selling online courses and people *I didn't even know* were giving me glowing feedback! I even managed at one point to get a 25% conversion rate on a webinar, which, if you know about these things, is not to be sniffed at.

Another learning was how to think about the best practice checklist I'd compiled. Instead of treating it like a set of rules, it became more of a set of guidelines. Which is, after all, what I'd compiled — the things that worked for most of the people, most of the time and a great starting point to experiment. There were always exceptions to break the rule.

This was the turnaround point — understanding that creating a course and selling a course aren't separate entities at all. Done properly, they are intrinsically linked. Done properly, they remove the pain and trauma of selling the thing you've spent countless hours lovingly creating. The selling bit is usually the part that terrifies most Subject Matter Experts.

This book is designed to give you exactly enough information about every aspect of designing, building and selling online courses so that you can replicate the process without the trauma. Some of this stuff will come more easily to you than others. The good news is, if you struggle with any bit, you will be able to be very focussed in what you are looking for and far less likely to suffer overwhelm.

As a trainer at heart and in action — my job, my purpose, my *passion*, is to take complicated things and turn them into easy to consume, bite-sized learnings. What that means for this book is that it can be a reference for you to return to time and again as you build and layer your knowledge around online course creation.

You might be tempted to skip to chapters that are of more interest to you right now. That will help you no doubt, but I encourage you to read through every chapter in sequence at least once, as there are references to the different parts of the book throughout. So, let's get on with it!

Ginette Tessier
May 2022

p.s. this book is written mainly from the point of view of creating and selling pre-recorded online courses to individuals. If you are intending to sell your courses to corporate organisations, most of the book is relevant to you as presented, but where you need to be thinking a little differently, I have provided some extra information for you.

p.p.s. extra resources for you:

- Get your copy of The Best Practice Checklist and lots of other helpful things by going to: **GetThatCourseOnline.com/Resources**
- Join my free online business community 'The Get That Gang' on Facebook.
- Sign up to the course that complements this book by going to **GetThatCourseOnline.com/Course** and also find out how to access ongoing training with me.

Pay attention to this if you want to sell courses

CHAPTER ONE

The Online Course Taker's Mantra

1

The Online Course Taker's Mantra is something I developed back in 2015, in response to the common mistakes I saw new online course creators making. It goes like this:

> Give me the information I want,
> Over as little time as possible,
> In a way that's easily accessible,
> At an appropriate price for the value delivered.

Each line represents a different mistake I saw being made, so let me explain what they mean:

Give me the information I want

As a subject matter expert, I'm sure you know your stuff. And the longer you've been an expert in your subject matter, the more you'll know — and have forgotten — about what it's like to not be an expert.

You probably have something called 'The Curse of Knowledge', which is a curious thing. Its point is to say that now you know so much, you aren't easily able to relate to those who know next to nothing about your subject.

In online course creation, this manifests in forgetting that although you know precisely what someone needs to know, they don't know what they don't know...

Stay with me here! When you, or anyone else, sets out to learn something, you often begin with a desire — a want — to have a question answered. That question is usually phrased something like: "How do I?" or "What is?"

This expresses what you want to know — because you don't yet understand what you need to know to have a good grasp of the subject in question.

Consider toast (trust me, this is going somewhere). Delicious, crispy, toasted bread, perhaps with a generous curl of butter, just at the point of melting into the surface and the aroma of salty warmth gently caressing your nostrils.

You've probably got a particular type of bread that's your favourite to be toasted — maybe it's seeded, sourdough, plain white, something else. Maybe you don't eat plain butter but prefer a slab of peanut butter instead.

Don't worry, I'll pause while you go make some...

Now put yourself in the shoes of someone looking to better understand how to make toast. Let's imagine for a second that they've heard about this delicious snack, maybe even tasted it, but they haven't yet had any experience of creating it themselves.

They don't know that they need to understand the different types of bread, toppings and even the ways to get the bread just the right level of toasted. What they want to understand is "How do I cook toast?".

That sounds a little wrong though, doesn't it? Technically you cook bread not toast, but in widely accepted English phrasing you would refer to the process as *make* toast.

Already you have succumbed to the Curse of Knowledge. How did you know to use the word 'make', instead of the word 'cook'? You already have the knowledge.

A simple example for sure, but now apply that to your subject area. Take it right back to the very earliest question you had about the subject. Did you ask something insightful and knowledgeable? Or did you make a small faux pas such as 'cooking' toast, simply because you didn't know any better at that point?

So why is this important to online course creation? Simply put, you will sell way more of your courses if you concentrate on understanding and providing what people want, rather than exclusively what you know they need.

You can definitely include what they need along the way. But keep the 'want' front and centre when deciding what your course is about and what you're going to include.

People search for what they want because they don't know what they need. People then usually buy what they want, but they don't always buy what they need. Sometimes these two things are one of course, but it's a very common mistake which, if you don't it get right from the start, will often end with disappointment in a lack of sales.

Over as little time as possible

Trust me when I say that no-one wants to be sitting in front of a computer screen listening to you (or me for that matter) for longer than they have to. Harsh but true!

That might feel a little unfair — after all, I'm unlikely to have heard your dulcet tones at this point. You may have the voice of an angel...

Let's assume for a second though, that you have an 'ordinary' voice. You can sound excited, sad, happy, angry — all the emotions. You're capable of holding lengthy conversations with friends. Maybe you've even had experience of speaking in front of groups of people. Maybe you finished to a standing ovation.

So why am I so sure that people don't want to listen to you for longer than they have to? At this point it would be easy to quote the stats around attention spans that are widely available on the internet. The astute (sceptical?) among you will know that they aren't quite as robust as they might be.

For example, the poor goldfish, often the target of attention span jokes, has a scientifically proven quite good attention span. But let's not let the truth get in the way of a good meme...

Somewhat surprisingly, there are not that many credible sources around attention spans. For example, the argument that they've reduced on average from 12 seconds to 8 seconds in the last twenty years isn't traceable back to any published scientific study. You can read my source for this by going to **GetThatCourseOnline.com/Resources**

But it feels right. It feels accurate. And the reason we attribute credibility to the feeling is that we can remember ourselves 'proving' it. We can remember bouncing off internet pages that don't load quickly enough, or are too annoying with advertising, or take so long to provide us with an answer, we get frustrated and 'x' out.

So, again, why am I so sure that people don't want to listen to you for longer than they have to? It's not because of attention spans at all. It's because you, at the moment, are highly unlikely to have developed the acting and film-making skills required to keep people interested and engaged for very long, unless it's directly relevant to what they want to find out.

Don't think I'm trying to separate us out here either — neither have I.

The last point I made about the attention span thing feeling right — that we can remember being frustrated with an internet page that takes too long to get to the point? Yeah. There you go. That's why people won't listen to you for more than they 'have to', unless you have mastered the art of only including the information that is essential to your course.

It's not because they don't like you. It's also not because the subject isn't riveting (although some of you might openly admit to not having the most exciting subject matter out there).

It's simply because we tend to think that we aren't providing value to our learners if we don't have a serious volume of information. And yes, sometimes, we will need lots of information to explain something complex. But often the reason for having a lot of information is not the content — it's the creator.

It astounds me that there are still course creators out there proudly boasting of their five, ten, or even twenty-hour courses. Personally, I can't think of anything worse than spending that long in front of a computer just to learn how to cook toast...

In addition to frustrating learners by not getting to the point quickly enough, there are another couple of reasons you don't want to make your course longer than it needs to be: speed and ease. There's nothing more attractive to potential course buyers than the promise of a speedy route to the top of Mount Knowledge — even better if there's an express elevator to get there.

By making your course as short as possible (while ensuring it contains value), you are tapping into a fundamental desire for speed and ease (a business mentor of mine sums this up as 'people are lazy'). It makes your course very attractive indeed — definitely more attractive than the competition inadvertently advertising 'difficult and slow' with their twenty-hour boast.

The next reason for ensuring you only include what's essential to delivering your course 'promise' (more on this later in Chapter Five), is so that you have additional areas to offer follow-on courses. These could be the next level of knowledge, or something at a tangent to your current course.

People who have bought from you once are much more likely to do so again — but they can't if you've already sold them everything you have!

Finally, the last reason for making your course shorter rather than longer is simply so that you can get it finished. This is especially important if you are embarking on creating your first online course.

You will start out full of hope and excitement, highly motivated to get it out into the world and start making some money. Then reality inevitably bites and you find out that online course creation has a bit of a learning curve. Not only that but filming all those lessons takes way more time than you thought.

When that point hits, you are definitely going to be thankful that you only need to complete nine lessons instead of forty-nine. It's a lot easier to convince yourself to plough on through and get it done.

In a way that's easily accessible

At the risk of stating the obvious, people signing up for online courses usually want to be able to take them. And yet there are still creators out there insisting on various hoops that need to be jumped through before that can happen.

Either an account must be created separately to the signing up or payment process, or some kind of form has to be completed, or sometimes even the course isn't released until a specific date for no apparent reason. Note that this is different to a deliberately designed drip-released course or one where all learners need to begin at the same time due to other factors.

Then there are the courses released on platforms that aren't mobile-responsive or can't provide subtitles or cater for screen-reading technologies. Ones that insist on a course quiz after every lesson (quizzes have their place, but not after every lesson); ones that only work if reams of downloads are printed off; ones that can only be consumed through a decent online connection.

Every step you place in the way of someone getting to the information they have paid for, is a step closer to them having an excuse to walk away — or even worse ask for a refund.

Now don't get the idea that refunds never happen — they do, for all sorts of reasons — but why you'd knowingly give people an extra excuse to ask for one is anyone's guess.

The point about making your course easily accessible is also about speed. When someone buys an online course, they are usually excited and motivated to start. The quicker you can help them to do that, the more likely they are to feel good about the experience. Feeling good about it then makes them more likely to come back to your course when they've completed their initial foray into the material. Very few people buy a course and then consume it all there and then.

It's a concept I call 'learner-led control' — if you're a class-based trainer of any kind, this will be the opposite of what you're used to. You will be used to setting the timings, including when people take breaks and when they knuckle down and get the work done.

Not so with online courses — you are at the mercy of the learner. They get to decide when they start, when they take a break, when they browse the socials instead of giving you their full attention...

You may be used to some of this if you have developed virtual live training of course (much more likely since the Covid-19 pandemic), but the design of virtual live training is still much closer to classroom-based training than it is to pre-recorded online courses.

In this respect, ease of accessibility also covers the way in which you design your course. There's much more on this later on in Chapter Seven, but at the risk of spoiling the surprise, you should know sooner rather than later that you are 99% certain to be designing lessons of a maximum of five minutes at a time.

One of the reasons for this is so that it is deliberately easy for learners to pick up the thread again after putting it down. They don't want to have to search for ages through a video to find the bit they stopped at before. The shorter your lessons, the easier it is for them to pick things up again (and review the last one they watched to get back into it).

At an appropriate price for the value delivered

Pricing online courses is a topic that pretty much consumes every creator at some point — even though some will eventually forget just how stressful this subject can be at the beginning.

There are a few important things to remember about this one, not least that there is NO set formula for calculating online course prices. I have been known to have a little bit of fun with this one when I'm training a live version of this book. See Chapter Thirteen for more.

Next to remember is that most of the time, the price of your course has only a very distant relationship to the length of your course. I've already given you plenty of reasons not to make your course too lengthy. Now that you know you don't price based on length either, hopefully that lesson is underlined for you.

The reality is that people are prepared to pay for an online course if it delivers what they want. And depending on the level of transformation they're looking for, they are also prepared to pay significant sums of money for it. I use the word significant quite deliberately there — it's subjective and therefore entirely in your hands.

Yes, pricing psychology is a 'thing' — you can read more about it through various reputable sources (I recommend some on **GetThatCourseOnline.com/Resources**). Suffice it to say for now that there is such a thing as too cheap. Do not be fooled into thinking that free courses are the way to go unless it's part of a very specific marketing strategy.

If you follow my recommendations for how to choose your topic in Chapter Five, then working out your pricing will be a lot easier, I promise.

CHAPTER ONE KEY POINTS

★ You will sell more courses if you provide what people are looking for instead of only what you know they need.

★ Don't try to cram everything you know into one course — it makes it less attractive to buy and cuts off any further opportunities for you.

★ Make sure taking your course is as easy and quick as possible.

★ Understand the value of the transformation your course provides to price appropriately. Remember price is rarely linked to length.

ACTIONS TO GET THAT COURSE ONLINE

- [ ] Write out a copy of The Online Course Taker's Mantra and stick it on a wall close to where you work on your course.
- [ ] Look at it often to remind yourself what's important!

Get a handy PDF download of all the chapter summaries and actions at **GetThatCourseOnline.com/Resources**

How to make sure you will definitely finish creating your course

CHAPTER TWO

The Online Course Maker's Mantra

2

For ages I only talked about the Online Course Taker's Mantra as a thing, even though I also helped people create courses using other mantras too. In writing this book, I felt it only fair to attempt to write a counterpart mantra for course creators.

I therefore humbly present to you, the Online Course Maker's Mantra:

> I promise to remember that done is better than perfect,
> Only fossils are set in stone,
> And that although the first is the worst,
> This doesn't mean it has no value.

Let's take a look at each of these as we did with the Taker's Mantra:

I promise to remember that done is better than perfect

There's a chance you've heard this one before, but that doesn't mean you can skip over it! It mainly tends to trip people up because they forget that when they are learning how to create online courses, they are learning a brand-new skill.

By the time you have reached expert-level in your chosen subject, you have probably forgotten what it's like to start as a true beginner. Most of what you learn now builds on what you knew before. It's very rare to learn something entirely new.

So instead of cutting ourselves a little slack, we tend to err towards beating ourselves up about getting things 'just right.' We entertain delusions of people critically examining our output and declaring us either the best thing since sliced bread, or utterly incompetent. This adds to the pressure of creating something perfect — it's a protection mechanism. How can we be an expert if we can't even create a course about our subject?

Let's see if we can put this one to bed for you. I say this full in the knowledge that it still almost trips me up every now and again (ask me sometime how many false starts I had with this book, even though it's the first one I've written).

I promise you — categorically — there is no such thing as a perfect online course. It's a unicorn. A myth. A fantasy. If you insist on clinging to the hope that you can produce something perfect — especially if this is your first go at it — then you might as well stop reading now.

It. Will. Not. Happen.

Striving for perfection leads you down a single pathway that never, ever ends. And if you don't finish your course, you can't sell your course. If you've pre-sold it (a technique I talk about later in the book), then you'll be owing a lot of people some money back...

The only thing you do by striving for perfection is create an ever-increasing probability that you'll never launch your course.

There are plenty of also-rans out there. People who started creating a course only to get stuck in a never-ending spiral of perfectionism. These are usually the people who claim that online courses are a waste of time. Don't be that person — buck the trend and get it finished!

Only fossils are set in stone

Aside from perfectionism, one of the biggest reasons I see people not finishing creating their course is indecisiveness. They reach a point where they need to make a choice about something — this structure or that one, this platform or that plugin.

I'm going to make you another promise here: it 100% doesn't matter what you choose. Why? Because you can always change your mind again later.

This is why I roll my eyes when I see yet another post in a course creator group asking: "What's the best XYZ?" I do understand why the question is asked, because people don't want to waste time or money.

But there is no such thing as the 'best' anything when it comes to online course creation. There's only what's right for you, right now. So whichever choice you make, it's right for you, right now.

If you want to do some research into the choice in front of you through social media, it's much better to ask something like: "Which is better for a beginner: X or Y?" At the least this forces people to vaguely consider putting opinions alongside their recommendations.

Otherwise, what you get are responses from people with either a vested interest in you going with their answer (beware unstated affiliate links or unsolicited direct messages offering to help you) or people who have no experience of anything other than what they're currently doing. 'Most mentioned' and 'best' are not synonymous.

And that although the first is the worst

This refers to your first online course — if you've already made at least one then you'll understand this immediately.

Remember I said that when you learn how to create an online course, you are learning a new skill? When was the last time you picked up a new professional skill and produced your best ever version of whatever it was at your first try?

If your answer is anything other than 'never', you may want to find a book on how to be a bit more honest with yourself...

The first online course that you create will inevitably be your worst because you've never done it before. So instead of spending forever at it, endlessly tweaking it, trying to produce something extraordinary, why not get the first one out of the way as quickly as possible?

That way you can get on with creating your second (which will be better) and then your third (which will be better again) and so on and so on.

Maybe you're thinking that one is enough — that you only have one idea and one course you want to create? That may well be true right now, but I would caution you that once you understand how to create an online course properly, you are also much more likely to want to do it again.

My best advice to you — to everyone I train in this stuff — is to treat creating your very first online course as less of an exercise in *producing* an online course, so much as an exercise in *learning* how to produce an online course.

The act of producing your first course will teach you so much about what you do and don't want to do, when you do it again. I've had people train with me who have finished their first course and wanted to get on with the second one immediately because they knew exactly what they'd do differently the next time around.

This doesn't mean it has no value

Just because I said your first course will be the worst, that doesn't mean it will be terrible! If you follow the methods I give you in this book, you will likely produce something that is both sellable and provides learners with the outcomes you have promised them.

Even in the act of creating a course simply to learn about creating an online course, you will still produce something. This will place you head and shoulders above the thousands of people out there (I'm not exaggerating) who start creating a course but never finish.

And besides, value isn't only in the price someone pays for your course. The value also lies in everything *you* learn along the way.

Which happens to also be a top tip for creating your course — try to get your learners to create something along the way. It may not be possible for your subject, but anything you can get them to do to put their knowledge into action while learning, will result in a much deeper understanding of the material and a better learner journey.

A better learner journey means a better chance of getting a great review when someone has completed your course, which is invaluable for then getting more learners. I talk more about course design and getting testimonials later in Chapters Nine and Fifteen.

CHAPTER TWO KEY POINTS

- ★ There's no such thing as a perfect online course and you can't sell or use a product that isn't finished.
- ★ Any decision you make in the process of creating your online course can be changed later down the line — you only need to decide on the best solution for you for now.
- ★ Getting your first online course completed helps you get the 'worst' one out of the way quickly so you can get on with getting better at it.
- ★ Whatever you produce, 'worst' doesn't equal 'terrible' — there will be value in what you create.

ACTIONS TO GET THAT COURSE ONLINE

- ☐ Write out a copy of The Online Course Maker's Mantra and stick it on the wall next to the Taker's Mantra!

Get a handy PDF download of all the chapter summaries and actions at **GetThatCourseOnline.com/Resources**

How to make marketing and selling your course one of the easiest things to do

CHAPTER THREE

Who are you talking to?

3

There's a lot of debate in course creation circles about this one. The poor old, much-maligned, customer 'avatar' or pen-portrait regularly takes a bit of a bashing from those who prefer to build first and find out who's interested in it second.

There's an argument for this approach — not one that I subscribe to — but it can certainly be a tempting route for those less interested in the content they are putting out versus the money they can see themselves making.

And while we're here, there's nothing wrong with making money from online courses. If you are not interested in making money, then you're running a hobby, not a business. There's equally nothing wrong with that either, as long as you're honest with yourself about what you're doing.

But for an expert like you, there's going to be a level of passion for your subject that means you likely feel deeply uncomfortable with the prospect of simply chucking something together to see where it lands.

There's another reason for not taking the 'if you build it, they will come' route too. The people usually going down that path are way more comfortable with the idea of marketing than most subject matter experts I come across. They already have the channels available to reach masses of people and are usually very comfortable with the "pile 'em high, sell 'em cheap" model of business.

But the people I work with, by and large, love the thought of sharing their knowledge. They love the prospect of earning 'passive' income. What they don't love — and will often actively go out of their way to procrastinate about — is the idea of marketing. Or even worse (say it in a whisper) *selling*.

Good news friends! If you follow the methodology in this book — the marketing and selling bit becomes one of the easiest things you will ever have to do.

As I noted in the Introduction (you didn't skip that bit, did you?), taking selling into account from the beginning of creating a course helped everything else fall into place so easily, I sometimes wondered if I was somehow cheating!

The very first thing I want you to do in the creation of your course is to think deeply about who you are creating it for. And when I say 'who' I mean a single person — preferably someone you already know.

This is important for two reasons: firstly, creating for a single person means you are less likely to get bogged down in the never ending 'what if' spirals; trying to imagine every possible personal learning scenario and then cater for it in your course.

The single person will have a set of 'ordinary' needs around your subject matter, which makes it much easier for you to discount all the outlier scenarios. The ones that you rarely (if ever) come across in your other ways of imparting your knowledge.

Secondly, if you can use someone you already know, you are much more likely to be yourself in the creation process.

Huh?

OK, I may need to break that one down a bit. For some reason, many of us seem to think that being ourselves when recording an online course is somehow not correct. We think that we need to suddenly look differently, sound differently, even talk about our subject differently. We create a whole new persona — which never quite feels right.

Because it doesn't quite feel right, we keep re-writing and re-recording our course, all the while telling ourselves we're "not trying to be perfect, honest", but never really feeling satisfied with our output.

I understand why this happens — it also happened to me initially. There's something more permanent about an online course. We can't cover off something that happens on the fly as we might in a live situation for example. A recorded video lasts for a long time, so naturally we want it to be representative of us on our best day.

Except we also have that little inner voice that says: "ah but you've never recorded an online course before, so you'd better find out how other people do it." And we look around for examples, find them from people who have been doing this stuff for years and start to question whether we could ever seem that confident on camera.

Inevitably we tell ourselves there's no way we'd ever be that confident and then invent another version of ourselves which isn't really us because it's based on how we imagine someone else to be. We end up feeling even more uncomfortable than if we'd just been ourselves in the first place.

But...

If we are creating for someone we already know, then it's less likely that we will try to impersonate someone else. They already know us, they didn't run away screaming when we started to talk (phew), so maybe, just maybe, we can get away with writing and recording as ourselves and it will be OK.

It will be, I promise. No-one will ever question or second guess you as much as you. It will be OK.

So back to this known, single person you are creating for. Imagine them in conversation with you, asking about your specialist subject. What questions will they ask? How will they phrase them? What problems will they think they'll have in learning the subject or putting it into action?

If you were training them to reach a specific point, what would they need to know and be able to show to say they've 'finished' the course? Is there a commonly accepted way of describing that status?

Write down the answers to these questions as best you can right now. As you'll see in the next chapter, you will also be able to go back and add to this information once you've done a bit more fact-finding too.

If you do this work now, I promise you the selling bit becomes really easy! But skip this bit and not only will your creation likely get bogged down, but you'll really struggle when it comes to pulling together your marketing messages too.

CHAPTER THREE KEY POINTS

★ Understanding who you are creating your course for makes the marketing and selling bit much easier.

★ Don't try to be someone else when creating your course – it's exhausting and won't feel right.

ACTIONS TO GET THAT COURSE ONLINE

- [ ] Picture the single person you are creating this course for.
- [ ] If you can, make it someone you already know and that knows you.
- [ ] Imagine yourself in conversation with this person and write down the answers to these questions:
    - What will they initially ask about your subject?
    - What specific language will they use?
    - What problems will they worry will hinder them in being successful in learning the subject or putting their knowledge into action?
    - What will they know and be able to show after completion of your course?
    - Is there a commonly accepted status they would be able to use after completing your course?

Get a handy PDF download of all the chapter summaries and actions at **GetThatCourseOnline.com/Resources**

Crucial information that will make people say: “Shut up and take my money!”

CHAPTER FOUR

How to find out what they want

4

Do you know how to ask a question?

That's an odd way to begin a chapter, I know, but it's a serious point. Let me elaborate: do you understand how to ask a question in a way that will produce a meaningful response? A response that will help you to understand what your audience *really* wants out of your online course?

As a very quick aside here, please don't assume that you already know what people want so you don't bother trying to find out what your audience are asking for. This is the quickest way to waste time producing a course that no-one wants to buy.

The more you know your subject matter, the more likely this is to happen if you skip the steps in this chapter. Remember I was talking about the Curse of Knowledge back in Chapter One? This is exactly what I was talking about.

Most people don't understand how to ask questions properly. They consider asking the question "What do you want?" to be enough and that somehow, we are all completely cognisant of the reasons behind why we buy things.

Unfortunately, very few of us truly understand why we buy what we buy. We'll rattle off a load of reasons why we *think* we've bought something, but these are rarely the real reasons. We tend to assume we've been quite rational in our choices, but the reality is that we are mostly driven by our emotions.

And without doubt, if you asked people what they wanted to know in your course, they'd give you some information that *might* be useful at some point. But you're the expert. You know already what information you *could* include. What we're trying to find out is what information you *should* include.

The information that will make people sit up and listen. The information that will make people say: "Shut up and take my money!"

That sort of information won't come to you through asking people what they want though. That information comes only through listening (which for our purposes also includes reading).

Most of us are quite poor at real listening. We're very good at filtering the words we hear and see through our own lens of experience and then interpreting what's being said into something that makes sense to us. We apply a level of evaluation to the meaning of the words too. NLP (neuro-linguistic programming) fans will be familiar with this concept.

This isn't necessarily a bad habit. It's a useful way for us to understand social etiquette and have conversational shortcuts. But when it comes to understanding what people are *really* going to pay money for — which is different to merely *saying* what they're going to pay money for — real listening is key to understanding.

It begins with finding out *where* people are talking about your subject. Even better if the person you are picturing from the previous chapter is already in that space. It could be an online discussion forum or group, it could be somewhere they regularly express their opinions or views, it could be a local networking event or perhaps even a podcast or talk radio show.

Wherever they are, you should be too. Not participating, simply listening. Make a note of the questions they have, the assumptions they're making, their responses to the answers they're being given.

When you've spent some time absorbing that, you are ready to ask a few questions of your own (always within the rules of the space you're in of course). Great questions seek to understand another person's point of view — don't fall into the trap of trying to second guess what they are thinking. Use open ended questions such as: "What's the most frustrating thing about learning how to X?"

The answers will not only help you to understand the common language used by those you are looking to help (remember, it's about what they want, which won't always be the same as what you know they need); the answers will provide you with rich information about the obstacles they see.

This will help you create an online course which is a solution to those obstacles. It will also help you easily appeal to the people who are most likely to buy your course. Think about this point for a second: if you create an online course that is the solution to the obstacle your audience is currently facing, how much easier do you think the sales bit will be? Exactly.

Understanding the obstacles is often referred to as understanding the 'pain-points.' What are the points of 'pain' (i.e. frustration, overwhelm, confusion, misunderstanding etc.) that your audience would happily pay for the solution to?

But what if your target audience aren't in a space where you can interact with them? Offhand, I can't think of an audience that wouldn't be reachable in this way, but just in case: have a look at book reviews on your subject — Amazon is a good obvious starting point.

If there are any well-known books on your subject (maybe you've written one or more of them), have a look at what the reviews are saying. What language is being used? What are any complaints about — especially where people feel there's information missing that they wanted?

You could also try something a little broader, such as allowing Google to complete a sentence for you. Open your favourite browser, go to Google and type in 'How do I' plus your subject, then wait for Google to fill in the blanks with its predictive search facility. This may also lead you to a space you'd hadn't previously known about, where your audience are hanging out.

And if you still can't find anywhere to ask questions or get information, but you are convinced there is a large enough audience out there for you to sell an online course to, why not start your own group?

If you are talking about a subject and enough people want 'in' on the discussion, you'll have a ready-made audience to listen to, ask questions of and ultimately market your online course to.

CHAPTER FOUR KEY POINTS

- ★ Never assume you already know what your audience want from an online course, if you haven't been properly listening to them already.
- ★ You are aiming to understand their common language and 'pain-points.'
- ★ Find out where they're hanging out — easiest online but can also be done in person.
- ★ Listen first before asking questions — and make sure those questions are designed to get them to elaborate on what they want.

ACTIONS TO GET THAT COURSE ONLINE

- [ ] Make a note of the language used and common 'pain-points' discussed by your target audience.
- [ ] If the space rules allow it, ask open questions designed to get them to elaborate on any pain-points.
- [ ] Go back to the questions you answered at the end of the previous chapter — what can you now add to your knowledge?
- [ ] If there's no online space for your audience, either make one, or use book reviews and Google auto-fill to help you in your research.

Get a handy PDF download of all the chapter summaries and actions at **GetThatCourseOnline.com/Resources**

5

Finding the why that leads to the buy

CHAPTER FIVE

Topic selection — titles and transformations

5

By now you are in a much stronger position to make a good decision about the specific topic of your online course. Ideally, you will have picked something that seems to be a common pain-point from your research. To make the point again about the importance of listening to your audience, know this: you will never have to work hard to convince someone to buy something they are already looking for!

Think about the learning range you want your learner to have — are you trying to take someone from beginner to expert (not advised for your first course)? Or are you giving someone the knowledge required to understand or achieve a specific piece of the overall puzzle?

This, and the rest of this chapter, will help you keep focus on what you're going to include in your course. But before we get into that, we need to consider two things — what is our course called and what is our course promising? And remember from the Course Maker's Mantra: only fossils are set in stone — this can be a working title and promise for the time being.

But hang on — aren't the title and promise the same thing? Well, they might be. But I would argue that you probably want them to be separated — closely linked, but definitely separated.

Let's start by understanding that a title is simply a short way of 'labelling' your course. Trust me that you will want to be able to easily refer to your course in conversation with someone who you know it can help. You also want something that's easy for people to remember, so it readily springs to mind when they recommend it to others. More on that later when we talk about marketing.

A title is a shortcut for your audience to understanding what your course is about — but might not contain the vital information that distinguishes your course from any others out there that have the same title.

Let's go back to our toast example from all the way back in Chapter One. We can easily come up with the title 'How To Make Toast.' Great. Simple, short and easy to remember. But it's not a promise of transformation. It's just a description of *what* they will find out.

It's not something that either distinguishes itself from another of the same title or engenders any kind of desire around looking into it further. It doesn't speak to *why* they want to know this. *And the why, is why they'll buy.*

A promise speaks to the (sometimes secret) hopes and desires that someone has in connection to the subject matter. Remember I said that very few of us are fully conversant with the psychology of buying? There are hundreds of books, articles, blogs and videos on this subject, so I'm not going to go off on a long tangent here. Although I'd recommend you put some time aside to learn more, as it's fascinating.

Just know that a promise offers to deliver those hopes and desires, even if there's a seemingly insurmountable obstacle in the way. Even if they've tried many times before and failed. Even if they've given up hope of ever being able to achieve it — whatever *it* is.

You may have heard of this as the 'transformation', or the 'outcome' or even the 'result.' Personally, I don't care what you call it, as long as you get what it is and why it's important. It's the promise you're making to the person buying your course: "By the end of this course, I promise you will be able to X."

Remember: your promise needs to be believable — it must be plausible. This is (at least partially) in the context of the length of time you're asking someone to watch your course for. For example, I don't for one second believe that I can become a celebrated Michelin-star chef with a chain of fully booked restaurants just by taking a ten-minute online course. But I would believe that I could learn more about making toast.

Of course, there is the argument that if someone doesn't know anything about your subject, how can they judge what an appropriate length of learning time would be? First of all, the people looking to understand your topic of expertise are likely to have more intelligence than a slice of bread, so they will be able to evaluate your course based on their experience of learning other topics of interest to them.

Second of all, it takes a particular type of person to create a course promising something outrageous in a ridiculously short period of time ('be a zillionaire overnight' territory). In turn they naturally attract a particular type of learner (for learner read 'gullible person'). There's a reason there's a cliché that says *A fool and his money are easily parted.*

You're not someone who falls into the latter category, are you?

So back to your promise. We're looking for the reason *why* someone wants to be able to know about your subject. What do they think this new knowledge will do for them? An online business buddy of mine once recorded a podcast episode with me and what he talked about is something that has stuck with me.

He said that when it comes down to it, there are only seven reasons why anyone buys anything. It's all about the belief of what the thing being bought will do for them. Sometimes there's more than one of the seven reasons in there, but there's always at least one. They are:

- *To make money.*
- *To save money.*
- *To save time.*
- *To save effort.*
- *To get a physical health improvement.*
- *To get a mental health improvement.*
- *To receive a social status uplift.*

You can search online and find many differing models around why people buy things. Having looked over most of the articles out there on this, I can fit everything into the above model and have found it to be the one that sticks best with me.

If you prefer another model you've found though, go for it. The point is to understand that motivations come from what we think we'll gain through a purchase. In the case of your online course, what do your learners think they'll gain by taking your course?

What was the last thing you bought? See where your motivation came from. Even something as lowly as a loaf of bread can be traced back to at least one of the categories. I'm serious! See how it could break down here. Think about why you chose the loaf you bought:

- *Make money:* perhaps you're making sandwiches to sell.
- *Save money:* maybe it was cheaper than the others.
- *Save time or effort:* buying a pre-sliced loaf.
- *Get a physical health improvement:* buying wholemeal instead of white.
- *Get a mental health improvement:* fresh bread is lovely — you'll feel good.
- *To have a bit of a status uplift:* buying the artisanal seeded sourdough to serve when the snooty relatives come round for lunch.

If you're still cynical about this as you always buy the same type of loaf every time, think about why you buy that brand instead of any other. Unless you always randomly pick up the first loaf you see, you are making a choice between two or more items. And that choice will stem from at least one of the seven reasons above.

Right about now you might be wondering how we're going to extract your promise from the information I've just given you. While I'm not suggesting that you use any of them specifically ('How To Make Toast: a sure-fire money-making opportunity!' intriguing, but no) it is useful to understand what the motivational drivers are with your audience, so that you can make a promise — in their language — that references these.

Your course could very well be around making or saving money etc., in which case lucky you. But it likely isn't, so you need to find the 'thing' they believe your knowledge will help them have, do or be. And knowing that comes from the listening we talked about in Chapter Four.

To begin with, let's see if we can do anything with our working title: 'How To Make Toast.' Imagine we know that our target audience isn't a complete novice — they know that you make toast rather than cook toast. Perhaps the addition of a qualifying adjective will do the trick: 'How To Make *Perfect* Toast.'

That's an improvement — but it still runs the risk of being a bit 'samey' to other options that might be around. And while we might argue that it now promises a transformation, it's still not quite strong enough to do the trick. It could do a bit more to persuade someone to look more closely at the contents.

The next step is to try to find the answer to the end of this sentence: 'So that...' In our example around toast, it might be: 'So that you can brighten your day with this delicious snack at any time.' This now feeds into a mental health improvement: brighten your day = feeling better.

Therefore, we now have a title and promise of: 'How To Make Perfect Toast: so that you can brighten your day with this delicious snack at any time.' This is both descriptive, plausible and speaks to a motivation — great!

You might feel that this still doesn't quite go far enough though — what if there is a big obstacle that they struggle to see past? Perhaps you need to explicitly spell out in your promise that this obstacle can be overcome by learning from you.

If that's the case, you can extend your promise with an: 'Even if...' This extension is designed to double-down on them recognising themselves in the promise and wanting to join your course.

The end of the sentence speaks about a common challenge your audience faces. Again, you need to pick something that the majority will recognise in connection with the first part of the promise. For the toast example, it might be something like: 'Even if you currently burn toast so badly the dog rejects it.'

Our full title and promise are now:

'How To Make Perfect Toast: so that you can brighten your day at any time with this delicious snack, even if you currently burn toast so badly the dog rejects it.'

Maybe you need to weave a couple of motivators in there — maybe your audience is motivated by a status uplift, but perhaps they feel their lack of money is an obstacle. The more time you spend thinking about how purchases map back to the motivations to buy, the easier this will become.

CHAPTER FIVE KEY POINTS

★ Think about the learning range for your course – are you taking someone from beginner to a higher level, or towards understanding a specific piece of the puzzle?

★ A course title tells someone what the course is about.

★ A course promise tells them why it's something they need – the why is why they'll buy.

★ There are seven motivations behind any purchase so you need to understand what the motivations are for your audience around your topic.

★ The 'So that… Even if…' extensions can help you define the promise.

ACTIONS TO GET THAT COURSE ONLINE

☐ Work out your title using the 'How to…' beginning if appropriate – remember this can just be a working title for now.

☐ Think about the promise of your course – what motivators can you speak to that will appeal to your audience?

☐ Write down as many different 'So that…' extensions and 'Even if…' extensions that you can think of. Which ones work well together?

Get a handy PDF download of all the chapter summaries and actions at **GetThatCourseOnline.com/Resources**

The easiest way to the Goldilocks amount of information to include

CHAPTER SIX

Finding your MVP: Minimum Viable Product

6

We've all done it. Started talking to someone about our chosen subject and soon got side-tracked by all sorts of interesting tangential side-notes that seem important to explain in the moment.

Sometimes we might even see the point at which someone's eyes glaze over. You can almost see the speech bubble above their head: "I wish I'd never asked!" No? Only me?

If you're expert in and enthusiastic about your topic, I'm going to bet the following: there have been times when your answer to a question strays far beyond the borders of simply answering the question. Don't worry, you're amongst friends here.

When we're enthusiastic about our topic, we want others to appreciate the topic too. We want them to see how brilliant it is. And this spills over into wanting to give them as much information as we can, because if they only knew what we know already!

Unfortunately, this well-meant intention can have the opposite effect — it can overwhelm to the point that someone actively rejects learning more. This is a common error I see and resulted in lines one and two of the Online Course Taker's Mantra: "*Give me the information I want, over as little time as possible.*"

We forget that it's taken us time to get to this point — our knowledge has been built up over years, perhaps decades, of learning. For online course creation, this means we need to find a way to ensure that we include only 'enough' information in our course to answer the question (our title) and deliver on expectations (our promise). We need to include the Goldilocks amount!

A useful way of doing this is to begin by listing out all the potential bits of knowledge that we could include. You can do this in any way that appeals to you — a traditional list on pen and paper, in a computer document, notes on your phone, a mind-map, flipchart and sticky-notes...

The options are many, so try a few out for size to see which works for you. Ideally you want something that's easy to play around with in terms of order and grouping.

You are aiming to chunk the information down into the smallest pieces possible. The reason for doing this is to make sure that we can achieve a balance and flow to our course. This is something I cover in detail in the next chapter.

For now, pick your technique and list/record everything you can think of. It can help sometimes to do an initial 'brain dump' and then come back to it later or add to it over the course of a few days, as your brain adds to the possibilities.

Let's use our work in progress around making toast to demonstrate the level of detail I want you to be thinking about:

How To Make Toast — possible inclusions:

- Buying bread
- Making bread — how
- Making — ingredients
- Wholemeal
- Seeded
- Soup and toast
- Who discovered?
- Grill/Broiler
- Egg and Soldiers
- Toaster
- Butter
- Olive bread
- Walnut bread
- Tomato bread
- Cheese on toast
- Jam/Preserves
- Marmite/Vegemite
- Toasting vs toast
- Dry toast
- White sliced loaf
- Tomatoes
- Mushrooms
- Bruschetta
- French toast
- When to have it
- Griddle
- Bloomer

And so on. Wow — who knew there was so much to think about with something as plain and unassuming as toast?

After the initial brain dump, you can start to assess the potential information against a simple scale, which is determined from your topic title and promise. In our case it is:

'How To Make Perfect Toast: so that you can brighten your day at any time with this delicious snack, even if you currently burn your toast so badly the dog rejects it.'

In the context of this title and promise, we assess each piece of information using the EDPO technique: is it **Essential**, **Desirable**, **Possible** or **Overkill**? Our aim is to get down to only the Essential information required to deliver the title and promise. We must be honest with this.

We might therefore look at our previous list and annotate it somehow (or create a new set of lists, or quarter up a flipchart page and use sticky notes — or however makes sense to you) like so:

E Buying bread	**E** Toaster	**O** Dry toast
O Making bread — how	**E** Butter	**E** White sliced loaf
O Making — ingredients	**P** Olive bread	**P** Tomatoes
E Wholemeal	**P** Walnut bread	**P** Mushrooms
E Seeded	**P** Tomato bread	**P** Bruschetta
P Soup and toast	**P** Cheese	**P** French toast
P Who discovered?	**E** Jam/Preserves	**E** When to have it
E Grill/Broiler	**D** Marmite/Vegemite	**D** Griddle
P Egg and soldiers	**D** Toasting vs toast	**E** Bloomer

Now let's group the items to make our lists easier to compare:

Essential	Desirable	Possible	Overkill
When to have toast	Toasting vs toast	Soup and toast	Making bread — how
Buying bread	Marmite/ Vegemite	Who discovered?	Making bread — ingredients
White sliced loaf	Griddle	Olive bread	Dry toast
Wholemeal		Walnut bread	
Seeded		Tomato bread	
Bloomer		Cheese	
Toaster		Tomatoes	
Grill/Boiler		Mushrooms	
Butter		Bruschetta	
Jam/Preserves		French Toast	
		Egg and soldiers	

At this point we can swap items between columns if we feel something isn't quite in the right place. We can add things too if we think of them now. There is no right or wrong here — just go with your instinct for what feels right.

We can see that we have spread toppings in both the Essential (butter, jam/preserves) and Desirable (Marmite/Vegemite) columns. At this point we might also remember that there are other popular spread toppings such as peanut butter or chocolate spread, so they probably need to be included too.

Given that we are adding a couple more items in, we might choose to put them in the Desirable column and probably move butter and jam/preserves over there too. For now, this is for no other reason than that column is shorter than the others. They may yet move back into the Essential column.

We will also want to spend a bit of time thinking about the other sort of toppings there are in the Possible column — are these items and the spread toppings all part of a bigger group? More on this in a bit.

As well as prompting thoughts for extra items, listing the potential items out this way tells us a lot of valuable information:

1. If we had simply started creating the course, using everything we could think of to include without doing this exercise, we would have easily run afoul of including too much information for what our course taker wanted. We would run a real risk of overwhelming them or making it look like we were 'padding out' the course.

2. The Essential elements of the course don't look at all daunting to create. We may even have capacity to include the Desirable elements without causing too much extra work or flooding the course with too much superfluous information.

3. Our Possible list is long enough, and filled with enough similar items that it could conceivably be another course itself — an interesting idea for a follow up course once we've established a fan base from this one.

4. The Overkill list shows us some information that might provide an option for another complete course or perhaps a collaboration with someone else with expertise in this area.

Our next step is to quickly do a sweep of the items in the Essential list, so that we are sure we have covered everything needed. At this point we want to refer back to the course title and promise again, just to ensure we keep that front and centre:

'How To Make Perfect Toast: so that you can brighten your day at any time with this delicious snack, even if you currently burn your toast so badly the dog rejects it.'

And in our Essential list we have (notice butter and jam/preserves have been moved out for the moment):

Essential	
When to have toast	Preparation
Buying bread	
White sliced loaf	
Wholemeal	
Seeded	
Bloomer	
Toaster	Process
Grill/Broiler	

Looking more closely at the items, it seems we have two core areas covered: Preparation (when to have toast, buying bread, types of bread) and Process (toaster, grill/broiler).

We might consider that 'buying bread' and 'types of bread' are probably the same thing — you can't buy bread without considering the type being bought. The type might also influence the process we use. There might need be a nod to where we buy our bread in there, but anything more than mentioning a couple of options will probably send that topic straight to Overkill!

So far, so good. Now let's reconsider the items in our Desirable list. If we were to include some or all of them, what impact would this have on delivering on expectations (the promise)?

On closer inspection, it feels like understanding the difference between toasting and toast is a fairly simple concept that we can deal with in an introduction to the course, so we can definitely move that into our Essential list.

Now let's consider those toppings. We might think that butter on toast is a minimum requirement of 'perfect' toast. To add in some popular spread options also feels like it would enhance the content, without causing overwhelm. So we can go ahead and move those into the Essential list.

The only item left on the Desirable list now is Griddle. This is a cooking method that is probably more closely linked to some of the items in our Possible list — for example Bruschetta. So let's make that decision and move it there.

Desirable	Essential
Toasting vs toast	Toasting vs toast
Marmite/Vegemite	Marmite/Vegemite
Butter	Butter
Jam/Preserves	Jam/Preserves
Peanut Butter	Peanut Butter
Chocolate Spread	Chocolate Spread
Griddle	When to have toast
	Buying bread
	Types of bread
	Toaster
	Grill/Broiler

This is great progress. We now have three areas to cover in our course: Preparation, Process and Toppings. This feels like it has the right amount of information to do the question and expectations justice, without being too much. We have found our MVP: Minimum Viable Product.

But what of the information in our Possible and Overkill lists? We have two outstanding thoughts to cover off here:

1 Should all the toppings (from our updated Essential list and Possible list) be treated as a distinct group of information? Are they actually another course?

2 Is there an opportunity for collaboration with someone who has expertise with the items in our Overkill list?

1 Should all the toppings be treated as a distinct group of information?

This is an example of how we can look at our brain dump of information in a few separate ways. Our options are to either add to the course as it stands with the additional toppings, or to consider the toppings in the Possible list as something different. Let's look at the Possible list again:

Possible
Soup and toast
Who discovered?
Olive bread
Walnut bread
Tomato bread
Cheese
Tomatoes
Mushrooms
Bruschetta
French Toast
Egg and soldiers
Griddle

Just isolating the toppings in that list (cheese, tomatoes, mushrooms), we can see that although they are technically toppings, they are a more 'advanced' addition to toast than a spread topping.

If we broaden the group to include Bruschetta and French Toast, then we can start to consider an additional option for inclusion in our course creation offer. Perhaps we can go further again and look at the 'toast plus' options such as soup and toast, or egg and soldiers.

Now things start to become interesting — there's a definite option here for another course called something like 'Advanced Toppings and Snacks.' We'd have a ready-made audience for it, with anyone who took the original course.

By removing the potential Advanced Toppings and Snacks from our Possible list (into a separate safe space to be thought about again later), we are left with the different types of bread and the question around who discovered toast. Griddle has moved with the Advanced Toppings and Snacks because it's a method to produce some of them.

Without the Advanced items in there, these remaining items are starting to feel more like Overkill. Or at least something more closely linked to bread rather than toast. That means we can move them to the Overkill list and answer our second remaining question:

2 Is there an opportunity for collaboration with someone who has expertise with the items in our Overkill list?

Let's review what we have in this final remaining list:

Overkill
Making bread — how
Making bread — ingredients
Dry toast
Who discovered?
Olive bread
Walnut bread
Tomato bread

It feels like going into the process of making your own bread is a step too far for our course — especially when we consider we have the word 'snack' in there, which implies quick and easy!

So now we have some thoughts around whether we could team up with someone who could or already has produced a course around making bread. Perhaps a joint venture would be beneficial for both sides? This is something we can explore, but again, we need to be wary of being side-tracked by this. Let's put this idea in another safe space for later — we'll discuss it again when talking about launching our course in Chapter Sixteen.

We have now reached a wonderful place in being clear about what we will and won't be including in our course. The next step then is to look at the structure of the course so we can make sure we have good balance and flow. In the next chapter I'll tell you what that means and why it's important.

CHAPTER SIX KEY POINTS

★ Including too much information in your course is just as bad as not including enough, so you need to find a way to reach your MVP: Minimum Viable Product.

★ When you have used a technique such as EDPO, you have a clearer picture of the options available, including additional opportunities to offer value and opportunities for promotion.

★ Being honest with using only the Essential items required to deliver on the question (title) and expectations (promise), helps you to stay focussed and efficient in creating your course. Not to mention delivering something your learners will love and appreciate!

ACTIONS TO GET THAT COURSE ONLINE

- [ ] Brain dump all the potential information you could include in your course. Do this in a way that works best for you — there's no right or wrong.
- [ ] Use EDPO to move items around between categories until you have a clear list that provides your MVP.
- [ ] Keep your Essential items to hand for the next chapter. Keep your Possible and Overkill items in a safe space for later.

Get a handy PDF download of all the chapter summaries and actions at **GetThatCourseOnline.com/Resources**

7

The difference between a so-so course and a great one

CHAPTER SEVEN

Outlining your course for balance and flow

7

After all the legwork we put in for the previous chapter, you might be wondering why we aren't just starting to film everything already. Yep, you could go down that path if you think you're ready.

However, if you really want to create something to be proud of, there are just a couple more steps to take before we get to filming. These can be the difference between a so-so course and a great one.

First up, we need to think about the course outline — do we have a balance and flow to the learning we are providing? This is about the amount of information we are including in each section and lesson. We want to have balance in the number of sections, the number of lessons and the length of each. By having balance, we will create a natural learning flow.

A natural learning flow will help keep our learners engaged and motivated to continue with our course. Ultimately, they are more likely to have a better experience and therefore tell other people about it — preferably in a video testimonial for you.

If 'sections' and 'lessons' are unfamiliar terms, you can check them out in Chapter Eighteen at the end of this book. For now, think of a section as a group of lessons providing information on a particular area. Lessons are the individual videos of information.

As a good rule of thumb, you should try to explain only one concept per lesson. Another great rule of thumb is to keep each lesson to five minutes maximum.

Yep, you read that correctly.

If anything, five minutes is almost too long in online course lesson terms. Remember line two of the Online Course Taker's Mantra: "*Over as little time as possible,*" We have been trained to expect information to be delivered in ever shorter bursts. Do you sit through the ads during YouTube videos, impatiently watching the countdown until you can skip? And that's only 5–15 seconds...

I know this is a point of resistance for many course creators. When I was learning about online course creation, I used to regularly skip over the bits of information I didn't want to believe, or (more often) didn't feel like doing the work for. Consequently, I learnt the hard way.

The world is not going to explode because your lessons are longer than five minutes. I'm sure you and I can both point to successful entrepreneurs who have online courses where their lessons are more like webinars.

However, I suspect those people have a solid online reputation and following already, so they don't necessarily need to operate with best practice in mind. Their fans will watch them whatever the case.

If you already have a great fan base who will hang off your every word, that's fantastic. But why would you deliberately risk their continued adoration? Why wouldn't you put in a tiny bit of work now to create something that *adds* to your already stellar reputation?

If you don't have a great fan base already, being this diligent now will help you grow that following.

> Note though, this is all based on the assumption that you will be using a delivery method that allows learners to proceed from one lesson to the next automatically — or at least with the minimum of interaction. I once took part in a course that failed in this respect.
>
> The problem was that it was delivered over an app that did not have an automatic 'play next' feature. Closing one video and having to click on the next one to open it up and then click again to get it to play became very annoying, very quickly.
>
> That combined with the course not having been designed in small chunks to begin with (it was originally a webinar that had been sliced up), made it a less than stellar learning experience. Don't worry though, we'll discuss the options open to you in Chapter Twelve, to ensure you get a delivery method that works properly!

Keeping your lessons short by design carries all sorts of benefits — for your learners and for you:

- Your learners will feel like they're racing through your content and therefore feel more positive about your course.
- They'll be eager to consume more as soon as they can — and they'll tell their friends about their great experience (hello referrals).
- They'll be able to find what they want very easily, watch it quickly and get what they need. This again adds to their positive experience.
- When they want to go back and check a particular piece of wisdom you have already imparted to them, they won't need to trawl through long videos to find it.
- You will also feel like you're racing through the process of filming your content.
- When you get questions, you'll be able to point learners to specific lessons that give them the answer. Trust me, there *will* be questions on stuff you *know* you've included in the course.
- Should you need to, you can easily update single lessons and just replace them quickly and easily on your chosen platform.

Now we understand the importance of keeping our lessons short, let's start to get into the detail of what we're going to be covering in our course. We decided in the last chapter that we had three broad areas to cover with our course on making toast: Preparation, Process and Toppings. These are our sections.

Within each section we have several items we want to cover — our individual lessons. We also need to think about how we are going to start and end our course. An Introduction section allows us to set expectations of what the learner will get. This backs up any marketing messages already given and helps us to inspire the learner to get started.

A Conclusion section allows us to guide them to a next step of our choosing. As we have spent the previous minutes in the role of instructor, our learners will be more open to our suggestions on this. We could guide them to taking another course from us or working with us in another capacity.

Let's plot out our sections and lessons in a grid to get clarity on how it looks currently:

	Section 1 Introduction	**Section 2** Preparation	**Section 3** Process	**Section 4** Toppings	**Section 5** Conclusion
Lesson 1	Welcome and Instructor intro	When to have toast	Grill/Broiler	Butter	How to find out more
Lesson 2	What you will get from this course	Buying bread	Toaster	Jam/ Preserves	Thank you and testimonial request
Lesson 3	Toasting vs toast	Types of bread		Marmite	
Lesson 4				Peanut Butter	
Lesson 5				Chocolate Spread	
Lessons per Section	3	3	2	5	2

By reviewing the number of lessons in each section, we can already see that there is an imbalance. We could simply rearrange everything so that the numbers are more even. After all, we have 15 lessons in total, so why not just put three in each section?

That would work if we didn't much mind which section a lesson went into. But for our toast-making purposes, it wouldn't make much sense to just move peanut butter into the Process section and chocolate spread into our Conclusion.

Our best first step is to have a look at what we have listed as individual lessons. We haven't yet given much thought to whether they really are individual concepts, or whether there's an opportunity within each section to do a bit of combining.

Let's begin our lesson review by remembering that we are striving for a lesson of a maximum of five minutes. Our first sweep should be to see if any of the lessons look like they would take either longer than five minutes to explain or less than thirty seconds.

Already we can see that our Process section is probably a little 'lightweight' in comparison to the others. After all, bread needs to be placed either under a grill/broiler or in a toaster machine and cooked until it becomes toast. Maybe these two lessons aren't individual lessons at all. Maybe we could add them to the Preparation section instead, as one lesson.

Or perhaps we might think them quite involved. We could consider that the art of making perfect toast involves knowing how to achieve just the right amount of toasting, depending on the implement used. To get that right, we might need to understand more about each implement.

	Section 1 Introduction	**Section 2** Preparation	**Section 3** Process	**Section 4** Toppings	**Section 5** Conclusion
Lesson 1	Welcome and Instructor intro	When to have toast	Grill/Broiler	Butter	How to find out more
Lesson 2	What you will get from this course	Buying bread	Toaster	Jam/ Preserves	Thank you and testimonial request
Lesson 3	Toasting vs toast	Types of bread		Marmite	
Lesson 4				Peanut Butter	
Lesson 5				Chocolate Spread	
Lessons per Section	3	3	2	5	2

For this course we decide to err more on the latter. Although we won't go into the history of toasting tools (this would be Overkill for sure), we do want to cover a bit of explanation about which tool is better for which type of toast we are making. It still feels a bit like padding to stretch to two lessons though. Let's come back to this one later.

For now let's turn our attention to the other lessons. Do we really need an entire lesson on buying bread? Surely, it's just a question of deciding what sort of bread we want and then finding the place to buy it?

This feels like a sensible route, so let's combine types of bread and buying bread, so now we have just two lessons in the Preparation section: When to have toast and Selecting our bread.

Notice the subtle change here of the lesson name too from 'types of bread' to 'selecting our bread.' This feels like it has a narrower focus than just 'types of bread', which could get quite unwieldy, so we'll go with that change too in the spirit of keeping the video length under five minutes.

	Section 1 Introduction	**Section 2** Preparation	**Section 3** Process	**Section 4** Toppings	**Section 5** Conclusion
Lesson 1	Welcome and Instructor intro	When to have toast	Grill/Broiler	Butter	How to find out more
Lesson 2	What you will get from this course	Selecting our bread	Toaster	Jam/ Preserves	Thank you and testimonial request
Lesson 3	Toasting vs toast			Marmite	
Lesson 4				Peanut Butter	
Lesson 5				Chocolate Spread	
Lessons per Section	3	2	2	5	2

This means we now have two lessons in the Preparation section and two in the Process section. But we still have five in the Toppings section. Time for a bit more focus there.

As we look at the toppings, we can see that we could have one lesson on savoury toppings such as butters and Marmite, and one lesson on sweet toppings such as jams/preserves and chocolate spread. This will also get us out of a hole when we realise we've forgotten honey as an option...

	Section 1 Introduction	**Section 2** Preparation	**Section 3** Process	**Section 4** Toppings	**Section 5** Conclusion
Lesson 1	Welcome and Instructor intro	When to have toast	Grill/Broiler	Savoury toppings (butters, Marmite)	How to find out more
Lesson 2	What you will get from this course	Selecting our bread	Toaster	Sweet toppings (Jam/ Preserves, Chocolate Spread, Honey)	Thank you and testimonial request
Lesson 3	Toasting vs toast				
Lessons per Section	3	2	2	2	2

Now we're really getting somewhere. We have managed to create a course with two lessons in each of the three central sections, plus two lessons in our Conclusion section. But what of the Introduction section? Will we leave it at three lessons?

By now, some of you will be itching to make this a two-lesson section too. I'm with you! So what can we do? Let's think back to our deliberations about the Process section. What we could do is include a lesson about toasting vs toast here and expand that a little to talk about getting the perfect mouthful of toast. When it's just the right level of crunch, temperature and combination of toast and topping.

To get that, we need to select the right tool for the job of toasting, which leads us to a lesson on toasting tools. This lesson then allows us to include the grill/broiler and toaster machine in a single lesson, which feels much more sensible.

Et voila! Now our course outline looks like this:

	Section 1 Introduction	**Section 2** Preparation	**Section 3** Process	**Section 4** Toppings	**Section 5** Conclusion
Lesson 1	Welcome and Instructor intro	When to have toast	Toasting vs toast, getting the perfect mouthful	Savoury toppings (butters, Marmite)	How to find out more
Lesson 2	What you will get from this course	Selecting our bread, including buying it	Toasting tools including Grill/Broiler, Toaster	Sweet toppings (Jam/ Preserves, Chocolate Spread, Honey)	Thank you and testimonial request
Lessons per Section	2	2	2	2	2

We have balance.

At this point it's worth saying that striving for balance is ideal, but not a deal-breaker. If you really can't rearrange things to find complete balance, then don't. Maybe you have 14 lessons over five sections and including something else would obviously be padding.

The point of this exercise is more to see if it's possible to get balance, rather than to not move forward until it's there.

I have created courses where there has been a symmetrical balance for example — two lessons in the Introduction and Conclusion sections, three in each of the middle 'core' sections.

I have also created courses where there is off-centre balance too. It's OK, I promise. Think of this as something to aim for but not be bound by and you'll be just fine.

A final note is this chapter is for those of you who are worried that your collection of Essential items doesn't seem to neatly fall into sections. Perhaps you have a series of steps that need to be followed. Or maybe you have individual techniques gathered together, that don't need to be followed in a specific order.

Don't panic! If you have for example ten individual steps, if each of those is just a five-minute video lesson on its own, then you effectively have one section with ten lessons. Technically twelve to fourteen lessons, depending on how you do your Introduction and Conclusion lessons of course.

If you have a collection of techniques, then your sections are probably the techniques themselves. Simply work out what level of detail you need to get to, so you can aim for the five-minute lesson guideline.

You don't have to have sections if it doesn't make sense to. You do have to have individual lessons though, so it might be easier to work out what they are first, then play around with how you gather them together — if at all.

If you're struggling to work out what your steps are, try articulating what the start and end points are first. Then work out what the rough halfway point might be. From there, work out the three-quarter and quarter points and after that it should be much more clear for you.

CHAPTER SEVEN KEY POINTS

★ Balance and flow in your distribution of sections and lessons — and lesson length — keeps your learners engaged and motivated.

★ You are aiming to keep lessons to a maximum of five minutes. This has lots of benefits for you and for your learners.

★ Achieving balance should never take precedence over the flow. You want the lessons to feel like they are logically placed.

ACTIONS TO GET THAT COURSE ONLINE

- [ ] Examine your Essential items list and start thinking about potential sections and lessons. Plot out the lessons in each section to see where there might be imbalance.

- [ ] Play around with the lessons and sections until you have achieved the best balance you can, with the Essential items you want to include. You might want to rescue some things from your Desirable list (or move some things over there).

- [ ] If you don't have natural sections, then one section with clearly defined steps of lessons is fine.

Get a handy PDF download of all the chapter summaries and actions at **GetThatCourseOnline.com/Resources**

8

How to stay on track and focussed with your creation

CHAPTER EIGHT

Lesson content – what are you talking about?

8

After sorting out the broad idea of which bits are going where in our course, we need to spend a bit of time thinking about what pieces of knowledge, or concepts, we want to cover in each lesson. Perhaps there are specific points you want to make, techniques you want to show or tools you want to mention.

To stop everything coming out in a bit of a jumbled mess, with tangents all over the place as you think about different things (which is how conversations tend to develop), you will need to have a structure to what you are covering.

Call it a running order, a lesson plan or whatever you like — it's a way of making sure you include everything you want to include, in a way that helps a learner to build their knowledge. Think of it like completing a jigsaw puzzle: the section titles are the corners, lesson titles are the edges. The quickest way to fill in the middle is to make sure all the pieces of a similar colour are in the same place!

We start by understanding the learning objective (or aim) of the lesson. For non-trainers, this may sound a bit jargony — sorry about that — but it's important to think this through. We will use this information to help our learners understand why it's important that they pay attention. We'll do this though in a way that satisfies that well-known acronym: WIIFM.

What's In It For Me?

You might think that buying the course makes it obvious: what's in it for you? Why you get to learn how to make perfect toast!

But don't forget the Online Course Taker's Mantra: learners want the information over as little time as possible. If they've not taken a course with you before, they won't yet have that trust that you aren't one of these 'pad-it-out' online instructors.

They will be starting each lesson — whether they are consciously aware of it or not — metaphorically (maybe even literally), with folded arms and an attitude of 'come on then, impress me.'

Eek! No pressure then...

For every section and lesson you have listed in your course structure (as laid out in the previous chapters) you want to make a note of its main objective. Is it there for background, laying the foundations for what's to come? Perhaps it offers a pivotal piece of information, without which they can't achieve the overall promise?

Let's do this for the lessons and the first section of our Perfect Toast course:

		Learning Objective
Section 1 Introduction		To help the learner know, like and trust me as an instructor and to inspire them for what's to come.
Lesson 1	Welcome and Instructor intro	To reinforce that they have made a good buying decision, and to give them belief that I can help them achieve the promise by being friendly and relatable.
Lesson 2	What you will get from this course	To inspire them to keep going straight into the course by 'teasing' what they will be learning about and what this means for them when they have achieved the outcome.

You can see that there's a specific reason for both lessons and this is wrapped up into the objective for the section as a whole. The next step is to do this exercise for every section and lesson in the course.

Wow. That seems like a lot, doesn't it?

Yep, no doubt this is not the sexiest part of online course creation BUT I promise that if you want to create a course that will keep your learners motivated and engaged, this is a necessary part of the process.

Like all new skills, at first it might feel cumbersome, awkward and time-consuming. However, the more you do it, the more it will become second nature. Here's another compelling reason too: the information you note down now will help massively when it comes to writing your marketing messages.

It also keeps you honest. We have already done an exercise to only include the essential information that delivers the promise. This is a way of ensuring nothing has slipped through that net.

And really, if you are asking people to spend their money with you based on the promise of helping them achieve something, why wouldn't you want to put a bit of effort into doing that?

After you have written in all your section and lesson objectives, you can think about any specific information you want to include in each lesson. This starts the process of knowing what you will talk about in each lesson.

You don't have to wait until you've completed the learning objectives — make your notes whenever inspiration strikes. I sometimes 'bullet point' anything I think of while compiling the lesson list or writing the objectives.

Noting what you want to include will help you to ensure that you keep your videos to five minutes or less. You'll get a feel for how much information you need to have in each lesson for that to happen once you have recorded a few lessons. You can then split or combine lessons as you need to, to maintain balance and flow and short lessons.

But what if this is your first time doing this stuff?

You can make it easier by giving yourself a 'template' for each of your instructional lessons. These are the lessons that sit in the sections between your Intro and Conclusion sections — the part of your course that tells them what they want (and need) to know.

A template gives you a structure for what you are going to include. It makes it easier to know your beginning and ending (surprisingly important if you've not done this before). This will stop you launching in at a random point or trailing off without a defined stop.

A templated structure in your lessons will also provide an unconscious flow for your learner. They will have expectations of how a lesson will be delivered and be looking out for information they are particularly interested in.

Here's a good starter template for you — refine as appropriate as you get more experienced. I've completed it using Section 2, Lesson 1, of our toast course (Preparation/When to have toast):

What to cover	Specific content
What's the lesson about	*When to have toast — appropriate times and places to eat it or offer it.*
Why is it important (WIIFM)	*Understand when toast is appropriate. Don't make a social faux pas by offering it at an inappropriate time.*
The first piece of knowledge	*Toast at breakfast.*
Next piece of knowledge	*Toast as a snack or comfort food.*
Final piece of knowledge	*When not to have or offer toast.*
Recap of what they've learnt	*When to have toast — appropriate times and places.*
What's coming next	*Bread selection for perfect toast.*

Just to reassure you, you don't have to have three core pieces of knowledge, or concepts, to get across in one lesson — it just happens to be that way for the example. Anything between one and five concepts is fine, noting that the more you have, the easier (and quicker) they need to be to explain.

Unsure about including a particular piece of knowledge? Go back to your lesson objective — does it 'fit'? Still unsure? Go back to your structure — is there somewhere else it could go? Still unsure? Go back to your promise — is it really an essential piece of knowledge to include? Hopefully now you can see why it's so important to follow the steps!

Think now about the timing of your lesson. How long will it take you to cover each of the topics? You can find out by timing yourself talking about it out aloud. This doesn't have to be a finished 'script' (more on that in the next chapter).

I reckon for the information we want to include, the timing is something like this:

What to cover	Specific content	Length
What's the lesson about	*When to have toast — appropriate times and places to eat it or offer it.*	10 secs
Why is it important (WIIFM)	*Understand when toast is appropriate. Don't make a social faux pas by offering it at an inappropriate time.*	10 secs
The first piece of knowledge	*Toast at breakfast.*	30 secs
Next piece of knowledge	*Toast as a snack or comfort food.*	45 secs
Final piece of knowledge	*When not to have or offer toast.*	60 secs
Recap of what they've learnt	*When to have toast — appropriate times and places.*	10 secs
What's coming next	*Bread selection for perfect toast.*	10 secs
	Total length of lesson (approx.)	**2 mins 55 secs**

See how the lead in and conclusion of the lesson are much shorter than the delivery of the lesson concepts? I want to make sure I am talking for longer about the important stuff. The lead in and conclusion are the equivalent of a 'warm up' and 'cool down' in a gym class — important but not the core.

In addition, I have suggested that the three pieces of core knowledge could increase proportionately in length. Naturally it is very convenient when I am making up the course for the purposes of example, but if you have the opportunity to do this, it also helps with learning flow.

Now's the time to do this for the rest of your lessons. Don't get caught up on being super-accurate. The two most important things are to have the outline of what you will be saying and a rough target for how long you will take to say it.

Remember you are again looking for balance — try to keep lessons of a similar length. This means within a minute or so of each other if you can, rather than to the second. If you can't achieve that naturally (or at least without too much effort), remember to keep each lesson to a maximum of five minutes.

You will get a feel for how long it takes you roughly to start up and sign off a lesson without sounding rushed, so if you need to play around with lesson length, it's the stuff in the middle that will need thinking about.

In the next chapter, we'll look at how to deliver your content in a way that brings it to life for your learners.

CHAPTER EIGHT KEY POINTS

★ To make sure you include relevant information in a logical order in your lessons, you need to create a lesson plan.

★ The lesson plan starts with understanding your section and lesson objectives.

★ It's useful to have a structure or template to follow for each lesson.

★ Once you have mapped out the lesson plan, you can roughly allocate timings to each piece of the lesson, so you can keep it balanced and within the five-minute maximum overall length.

ACTIONS TO GET THAT COURSE ONLINE

☐ Write out your learning objectives for your sections and lessons.

☐ Create a lesson plan for each lesson following a template.

☐ Allocate timings to each part of each lesson to keep an eye on lesson length.

☐ Try to achieve balance with the lesson lengths, remembering that a clear idea of lesson content and a five-minute maximum overall are the main goals.

Get a handy PDF download of all the chapter summaries and actions at **GetThatCourseOnline.com/Resources**

Your learners hold the cards, but this is how you stack the deck

CHAPTER NINE

Lesson structure — how to train not drain

9

If you've ever attended any kind of training during your life — work or hobby-related — you will have, without a doubt, experienced the utter boredom and frustration that comes from listening to someone drone on for hours because they think 'training' means 'talk at you.'

You may have also been subjected to that ever so special variety of 'trainer' who reads everything off of a soul-crushingly full PowerPoint slide of text...

BORING! And the quickest route to refund requests and poor reviews too.

While I am a huge fan of PowerPoint done well, and will advocate its use in this chapter, let's be very clear here: if you think you need to write everything you want to say on a PowerPoint slide and then all you have to do is read that out to train your learners, we can't be friends.

Nope, not even if you bring me salted caramel Häagen-Dazs. Although I will obviously keep the ice cream to teach you a valuable lesson. For research purposes.

Phew — now that's off my chest, we can concentrate on how to produce lessons that are engaging and motivating for your learners.

The first thing to be aware of when designing lessons for an online course is the concept of 'learner-led control.' This is shorthand for understanding that your learner holds all the cards when it comes to deciding when to play, pause, stop or continue your course.

This is obviously a great benefit to the learner. They can pick you up and put you down in accordance with their other commitments, their personal preference for how to consume online learning and of course the big one: whether they find what you're saying interesting enough to keep listening...

Designing your lessons becomes that much more important when you have no say over how they will be consumed. You might have the most amazing final two minutes of a four-minute video, but if the first two minutes are dull, dull, dull, they may never get the attention they deserve.

So how do we make sure our lessons are engaging?

One of two things normally happens for people new to recording online courses — they either massively over or underestimate how long they will take to talk about something. Sometimes this can lead people to thinking about using a script. After all, you can't go too far wrong there if you're reading something out, can you?

If a script is something you have used before and are comfortable with, then go for it. Personally, I have found that using a script makes me feel conscious and stilted. Consequently, that's how my delivery comes across.

I prefer to use my slides to prompt me into talking about a specific point. If I have constructed my slides well, then I can build up layers of knowledge through what I'm saying and what the learners are seeing.

Slides aren't the only way to get information across of course, so let's spend a bit of time understanding your options. In order of ease to produce:

1. **Audio Over Slides:** where you are talking through each slide as it appears.
2. **Screencast:** where you are talking over a visual of something being done on screen (most often employed for showing how to use software).
3. **Screen in Screen:** like Audio Over, but you are on camera in a box or circle in a corner of the screen as well as seeing either slides or a software.
4. **Talking Head:** where you are seen on camera, most often talking directly to camera, sometimes with annotations on screen to underline key points.
5. **Talking Head plus Audio Over Footage:** a bit like a documentary where sometimes you are on camera and sometimes you are talking over relevant footage.

6. **Audio Over Animation:** where you, or a voice artist, is talking over animated video such as doodles, cartoons, or stop-motion animation (these can also be bought in, in pre-produced 'scenes', rather than produced from scratch).

And you can do a combination of some or all of the above. I have produced eLearning that has combined elements of Audio Over Footage and Animation. Most of the courses I produce for individuals to take are a mix of Talking Head and Screen in Screen.

If this is your first online course, I would strongly advise that you choose Audio Over Slides, with a small amount of Talking Head if you're feeling confident on camera. Remember your first one is about learning how to create a course more than anything else, so take the easy option.

As a rule, I suggest using Talking Head in your Intro and Conclusion and then Audio Over Slides or Screen in Screen for your instructional sections. This is because seeing you on camera will help your learners feel a sense of connection to you. They will be able to imagine you speaking once they have that mental picture in their head.

This will help to deepen their learning. Our brains respond well to mental imagery in learning. Knowing what you look like when you're speaking, enables the brain to feel comfortable listening to what you're saying, rather than trying to imagine what you look like at the same time.

You might be wondering about not having audio at all, just slides that either auto-animate through or rely on the learner to click through. Please be very clear on what I'm about to say:

THAT IS NOT AN ONLINE COURSE.

If you are asking someone to simply read through text on a slide, then it's an eBook. Nothing wrong with an eBook at all (you might be reading this in that form), but please don't try to sell it as an online course! And if you do, then frankly you deserve the refund requests coming your way...

For the rest of this chapter, I'm going to assume that you are using slides in your video lessons. Whether you're using PowerPoint, Keynote or some other slide-producing software such as Canva, the rule is pretty much the same:

You want to have something on screen changing at least once every thirty seconds or less.

This will help to keep your learners engaged with what's going on, because their brains will be anticipating something changing and stay alert to it.

Next time you watch any kind of TV show, actively notice how quickly the scene in front of you changes angle. Either the camera is panning or the angle changes — even for a few seconds. If you haven't done this exercise before, I think you'll be surprised how you haven't noticed how often what you're looking at changes.

It's the same principle for your slides — you need to change up what's on screen to keep interest going. You could either have one slide per 30 seconds (or less), or you can make use of in-built animation effects.

Just a note on animation though — less is more when it comes to the variety of animation styles you use. Keep it simple with either an 'appear' or 'fade in' effect. Otherwise, it just looks amateurish and confusing.

I went through a big phase of bullet points and I still bust them out on occasion as they prompt me for what I need to talk about. However, I have been guilty of overplaying the effectiveness of using bullet points, so these days I tend to use more of a mix of pictures, icons, animations and yes, still some bullet points.

For each of your lessons, think about the best way to get your concepts across. Would a good picture paint a thousand words for you? Is there a piece of video footage that shows what you're talking about? Do you need to build up a list or table on the screen, or perhaps a flow chart?

Helping people to 'see' or 'visualise' a concept is vital. Even if you are talking about something that feels straight-forward, such as placing bread in a toaster machine. Showing footage of the thing you are describing happening will have a greater effect on learning, than saying it alone.

While we're talking about pictures and footage, please make sure that anything you use in your online course is royalty or copyright free. Swiping images from Google or video from YouTube is not the way to go unless you have deep pockets and miracle-worker lawyers...

If you have PowerPoint on a professional license, there is a load of decent quality stuff available now that you could use. It's fine to use it if it's within a Microsoft product. You can also try some royalty-free sites such as pixabay.com or pexels.com. If you want some excellent quality images or footage, it's worth investing in software that gives you those things too such as Adobe Stock.

With all these options, you are responsible for making sure you have the right permissions for use. There's always the option to draw something yourself if you have the talent and the inclination. Many course creators I know get frustrated at not being able to find exactly the right image — so they draw it themselves.

Keep in mind that whatever you choose to put on your slide, you are trying to build up the levels of knowledge for your learner. You can help the learning effect by tapping into our natural affinity for wanting to see things become whole or complete, such as seeing all the steps of a five-point framework or a three-step process. Imagine how frustrating it is to be told there's a three-step process, but to only be given one step!

If there isn't a natural framework or process to hang the lesson on, think about using pictures or footage to display the 'incorrect' or 'correct' behaviour.

> **Pro-tip:** to reinforce what's incorrect, show black and white footage or pictures; to reinforce what's correct, show colour.

And yes, if you have a list that needs building, you can use bullet points. Just not too many (and build them up one by one using animation).

Play around and have some fun. If it's not fun for you, then the chances are it's not going to be much fun for your learners. Think about the subject matter and the appropriateness of what you're saying and showing of course, but generally being playful with this stuff will be more successful at keeping your learners engaged, than being stuffy and strait-laced.

Next up, we will look at some added extras you can offer in your course to complement the video lessons you are giving.

CHAPTER NINE KEY POINTS

- ★ Learner-led control means you have to work at creating interesting visuals for your learners.
- ★ There are broadly six types of lesson delivery you could use, with Audio Over Slides the easiest to produce.
- ★ There must be a voice element in the lesson, otherwise it's not an online course.
- ★ Bear in mind the need to give your learners appropriate visual stimulation through pictures, video footage, graphical devices or bullet points.

ACTIONS TO GET THAT COURSE ONLINE

- ☐ Decide what type of delivery you will have for each lesson.
- ☐ Build your slides by playing around with ways to complement what you are going to be saying.
- ☐ Don't be afraid to have fun! As long as it enhances rather than distracts from the point you are making, it will work.
- ☐ For any pictures or video footage you use, remember you are responsible for ensuring you have the right permissions to use them.

Get a handy PDF download of all the chapter summaries and actions at **GetThatCourseOnline.com/Resources**

10

Five ways to easily increase the perceived value of your course

CHAPTER TEN

Extras to aid learning and add value

10

Quizzes

"Oh, but there must be a quiz at the end of every lesson!" My eyes rolled and I might have let out a teeny-tiny, exasperated sigh.

"Why?"

"Well... erm... because that's what other people do!"

Aha.

There's an awful lot of opinion on the internet about how quizzes are the answer to everything when it comes to the effectiveness of an online course.

And I disagree with most of it.

Lots of articles quote 'vast amounts of research' around the efficacy of quizzing, but very few offer links to relevant research, that is conducted with adult learners of online courses. Most of the research is focussed on using quizzes in a children's academic environment. The rest focusses on providing information for the teacher to adjust their focus depending on what their students are (or aren't) retaining.

Neither of these scenarios are relevant to providers of online courses. Your course is set and recorded, so regardless of a learner's quiz score, your training remains the same. Does this mean you shouldn't include any quizzes? And if that's the case, why do so many platforms bang on about their quizzing capabilities as a benefit?

Well, it's like anything related to online course creation (or online business in general). If it has a job, you can measure whether it's doing what it needs to do. If it doesn't have a job, then it's a waste of time. Don't get me wrong here. I love a quiz, I really do. But not just for the sake of having one.

When deciding whether to include quizzes in your course, have a think about what you want it to do. Is it important that your learner commits certain pieces of knowledge to memory, or important that they understand how that knowledge fits within the overall topic?

If the first, then a quiz may be a good move. If the second, then you might be better off providing them with a task to complete. You might even consider that simply providing a 'cheat sheet' is a better move — skip ahead to where I talk about Downloads in this chapter for that one.

You can of course include quizzes just for a bit of fun — this can work well if your subject matter is at the more frivolous end of the scale and you want to provide learners with some nice trivia to bring up at their next dinner party (does anyone go to those anymore?).

Another reason to include a quiz is if you intend to adjust or update your course based on any results. Perhaps learners are consistently getting confused with a particular set of concepts (evidenced by a high percentage of incorrect answers to your end of section quiz). This will tell you that there is more to be done to explain the concepts, so you could focus on recreating that portion of the course.

If you have a platform for your course that includes quizzing capability, you will probably be able to offer two types of quiz: multiple choice and true/false. If you have the option to include text-based answers, my advice is don't! Unless the technology is extremely sophisticated (or you are deliberately testing someone's spelling ability), this will become far more trouble than it's worth.

For both types, the question element needs to be clear — unambiguous in what it is asking. For multiple choice, the incorrect answer options should be plausible — around three to four options in total. If they're not plausible, the quiz becomes a parody and therefore of no use as a learning aid.

For true/false questions, avoid using negatives or questions that contain too much 'wiggle room.' For example: "Is January not a month containing 30 days?". The answer to this could plausibly be both true and false: "True — January is NOT a month containing 30 days, it has 31.". "False — January IS a month containing 30 days, plus a 31st day.".

Don't think people will be that petty? Okaayyyy...

If you wanted to, you could have a quiz at the end of every lesson, but I think that's going overboard and will soon annoy your learners. Stick to one at the end of every section (not your Intro and Conclusion) if you're going to have them and keep the length to no more than five questions.

As long as you have a solid set of reasons for including a quiz, a clearly defined job for the quiz to do and a way of measuring whether it's doing that job, then include a quiz. If you don't, then don't!

Downloads

A fantastic way to add value to your online course is to provide some downloads for learners. There are broadly seven types:

1. **Cheat sheets:** these are usually lists or aide memoirs on a single page that learners can print out and pin up in a prominent place to help them remember salient points. It helps for any situation where a quick reminder of a sequence or explanation of a concept is handy. For example, find a course creation steps cheat sheet at **GetThatCourseOnline.com/Resources**

2. **Templates:** these are usually where a 'fill in the blank' style of information is given, such as templates for emails, where the relevant details are left for the learner to complete as appropriate. They help for any situation where providing a ready-made item would be highly valued by the learner as it will save them both time and effort.

3. **Swipe files:** these are usually a collection of examples to illustrate a point being made. They are most often examples of good practice or examples of bad practice and all designed to show how pervasive something is, or to offer inspiration for a learner to complete their own version. Be aware that there may be copyright permissions you need to get — even for publicly available material.

4. **Worksheets:** these are usually documents that are provided with individual lessons, where it would help a learner to record their findings and thoughts in a more structured format than their own notes. They help to embed learning by providing a means to physically write things down. As this uses another sense (feel or touch) and different brain power, it can create a stronger attachment to the concepts being explained. You can provide electronic

worksheets only, but I would advise having a version available for people to print off. We like something tangible in our hands!

5 **Workbooks:** where every lesson has its own worksheet, an overall workbook can be a good option. This can also provide learners with a sense of tangibility and connection if the workbook is provided at the onset of a course. Having a workbook reinforces their progress and helps to maintain motivation.

Pro tip for worksheets and workbooks: your PowerPoint slides could easily be converted here to either be the basis of worksheets or produced as a PDF with 'notes' pages for learners.

6 **Calculators/calculation tools:** these are usually an Excel file or similar with a little bit of formulae added in that allow learners to type in a value or other set of data. The calculator then produces an 'answer' which alters depending on what values have been used. This can be useful where you want to illustrate the correlation between inputs and output. I've also used them to create inspiration for course titles and promises — you can find this very basic spreadsheet at **GetThatCourseOnline.com/Resources**

7 **Apps:** these are effectively the more sophisticated version of a calculation tool and can also be used to help learners to track their progress in a particular venture. Popular with courses that require a habit to be built such as money tracking or weight loss.

If you decide to add downloads into your course, you can present them as a 'bonus' to the course itself — more about this at the end of this chapter.

Make sure you don't treat them as an afterthought — they should be subject to the same level of care and attention in their presentation as you give to your course. Make sure the branding is aligned and that you have considered printing in both colour and black and white (if relevant).

Equally, don't allow the production of a download to become a reason for procrastination. If you would love to provide an app, but don't have the first clue how to create one, then don't make your first online course launch dependent on having one. It can be a powerful addition later on (and a great way to re-engage learners).

Support

I'm often asked about whether a pre-recorded course should also have a 'live support' element to it. This is asking the question from the wrong angle though. It's not about whether the online course should have it — it's about whether the learner should have it.

What will a live element add? What shape will that live element take? How will these things affect the learner's experience? How will they affect the learner's expectations?

There are pros and cons to adding in a live support aspect to your online course 'package.' For true 'passive' income of course, you wouldn't have anything at all! However, there are some good reasons to do so — in a way that sets some clear boundaries around both your time and its purpose.

First of all, let's consider what form the live support aspect could take. You might want to offer one of the following:

1. **Lesson comments:** where you have a facility for learners to add a comment to any lesson in your course, which provides them a way to ask a clarifying question.

2. **Email support:** where you provide a dedicated email for learners to send in any questions, with an auto-response outlining the timescale for response.

3. **Course community:** where you have a 'safe space' for all learners to mix and mingle. The size of the group usually determines whether you might need help in moderating it.

4. **Dedicated 'drop in' sessions:** where you invite learners to meet with you online at specified times, so they can ask any questions and have you answer them.

5. **Planned live 'spotlight' sessions:** like a drop in, but where you have a specific aspect of your overall course that you are going to concentrate on for the length of the session. You could also choose to encourage 'off topic' questions in this space.

Just as with quizzes, there's no right or wrong here — simply an assessment of what will be of most benefit to your learners. It also needs to be something you are prepared to commit to. Have a look at the information below for ideas of some of the pros and cons of each:

1 Lesson Comments

Pros Gives learners a place to express their thoughts and ask any questions.

Cons Needs you to be consistently checking for any recent comments and to answer any questions within a reasonable timeframe. Learner expectations of a reasonable timeframe can often be unreasonable...

2 Email support

Pros Gives learners a focussed outlet for their questions. Easy for you to get notified of any questions.

Cons Emails can be lengthy and depending on the learner, not always clear in what's being asked. Can lead to lengthy email exchanges where you are trying to clarify what they're asking.

3 Course community

Pros Can provide a safe space for you to broadcast messages to your learners. Can be a valued additional asset for learners to feel safe in asking questions. If within an established social media space, easy for learners to stay engaged with you and the course. Provides an effective way to announce course updates or new courses for them to buy.

Cons You will need to spend time building the community and getting people to engage. Effective community moderation can get tricky the larger a community grows. You may need to employ additional admins or moderators to help keep on top of questions, comments and protect the group rules. Other learners may provide incorrect responses or even use the group to build their own community. You will get trolls — be prepared to deal with them (delete and block is usually the most effective action).

4 Dedicated 'drop in' sessions

Pros Lets you be in front of your learners in a controlled space so they can feel a greater connection with you (more likely to learn and buy more from you). Allows you to easily clarify questions so you are giving the most appropriate answer. Allows other learners to benefit from the answers you give. Can be a great way to troubleshoot any issues too so learners feel 'heard' (and don't vent on social media instead). Depending on an expected length to completion, you could choose to do weekly or monthly sessions.

Cons Unless you specify advanced registration, you have no idea who or how many learners may turn up or what they will want to know or say. Needs good facilitation skills to keep on topic, answer questions and keep within the time set. Must state some clear boundaries and expectations for when the sessions will run, how long for and what is appropriate to bring into a session. Can be taxing promising weekly sessions when you have few people initially taking your course or turning up. Tech always goes wrong at some point! Needs consistent publicity to remind learners it's available.

5 Planned live 'spotlight' sessions

Pros All the benefits of a drop in, plus allows you to dictate the specific topic of a session. Doesn't require new training to be delivered — can be specific to a lesson within your course. Learners feel they are getting additional value for money. Ideally done monthly.

Cons Must state some clear boundaries and expectations for when the sessions will run, how long for and whether you will be taking off-topic questions. Need enough depth to the course to run several sessions before repeating content. Needs good facilitation skills to stay on topic. Don't run them any more frequently than monthly, otherwise learners will use this as the course instead of the actual course and you will be saying "this is in the course" a lot. Tech always goes wrong at some point! Needs consistent publicity to remind learners it's available.

As a rule, I would advocate that the shorter your course, the closer to the start of the list your support should be and the longer your course, the more you will benefit from providing options towards the end of the list.

It's common these days for there to be a learner-only community group provided for an online course. You don't have to do anything more complicated than set up a Facebook group (or other platform depending on where your learners hang out).

There are options for off-Facebook communities — Mighty Networks, Circle, Discord and others. However, unless you have a strong community that are dedicated to being in each other's company, going off-Facebook is not recommended to begin with. This is simply because your learners won't be in the habit of being there and you are likely to only attract those who want to complain about something.

Yes, I know there is an argument about not allowing Facebook that level of control over your assets BUT until you are a more compelling proposition for your learner than coincidentally being on Facebook, you may have to live with that risk.

You will also likely come across learners who say they don't like Facebook and refuse to set up an account just to be part of your community. You do not have to provide an off-Facebook community because of this. They are entitled to their choice and you can make it clear that being on Facebook is not an essential part of the course. This should deter anyone from arguing they should have a reduced price because they don't do Facebook. More in Chapter Thirteen.

And if you don't do Facebook? Well then that's also your choice. You don't have to provide a community there. Just be aware that it will be unusual these days to not have one at all.

A final postscript on this point: if you are creating a course with the intention to sell it into organisations rather than to individuals, creation of a community might either be inappropriate, or it might be out of your control (perhaps the organisation has an internal community platform).

Similarly, if the organisation is taking your course and providing it on their internal systems, you may not have access to answer any questions. You could offer to provide some additional follow up sessions as part of a blended programme, but I wouldn't offer these as a 'forever' option — make a small number of sessions a specific offer with a definite cut off point, after which they have to pay you more money!

Bonuses

I mentioned bonuses earlier in this chapter as a potential option for your downloads. Think of them as extra bits you add into your offer (the total package that you are asking for money in exchange for). It's a bit like buying a car and getting the first year of tax or insurance thrown in for free — 'sweetening the deal.'

It doesn't have to be second-hand-car-sales sleazy though! If you are providing things that your potential learner will perceive to be a valuable addition to the offer, these can make a difference to the attractiveness of it. They can be the difference between buying immediately and taking a bit longer to consider options — which can of course lead to not buying at all.

Your bonuses should feel carefully considered — so don't chuck a load of other online courses in there and think that'll work. They need to feel like they complement your core product. You want to avoid including things that look like they are compensating for a deficit in the core product.

An example of that would be for our Perfect Toast course, if we didn't talk about the toasting methods, but included those as a 'bonus' set of videos. From the course title and promise, anyone sensible would expect them be in the main course in the first place, so adding them as a bonus feels like we're trying to make up for a shoddy original product.

While you can include a secondary online course as a bonus, generally it's better to avoid including something of the same delivery method. This is why templates, cheat sheets and swipe files are good additions. Calculators and apps as mentioned earlier work well too if they enhance the original product.

An easy option that many fall back on, is to include some time with you as the instructor — a coaching session or similar. There's nothing wrong with this, but a better option I would argue is to offer time with you as an upgrade option (they need to pay more to add it on), rather than a bonus thrown in. This ensures that time with you in person is seen as what it should be: a premium product.

If you have something that is springing to mind immediately when you are creating your course, then great. If not though, don't use this as an excuse to procrastinate. You don't need to have bonuses to offer with your first (or even second) online course. I don't think I offered any for at least my first five courses!

Certificates

Never underestimate the perceived value of a certificate. It's not something that has ever bothered me personally (the accreditation is enough), but for some people, having that smart piece of paper to put in a frame is a huge deal.

You don't have to have your course accredited by a formal industry body to award a certificate. I used to give out a certificate of 'completion' — it literally just said that someone had attended the course. It doesn't confer any qualification, or right to any letters after a name, but it is proof that someone has at least been exposed to something about the subject!

Your course hosting platform (discussed shortly in Chapter Twelve) may offer an automatic completion certificate option, or it might be available as an 'add on'. If you train people to receive a formal qualification that comes with conferred rights or abilities, check with your awarding body about how your online course material might fit into their framework. You never know, this could be an opportunity for you to sell in an online version to them.

Certificates are probably the easiest way to add perceived value to your course without much additional effort on your part. They won't affect anyone for whom they are not important, but they will be a big plus point for people who like them.

CHAPTER TEN KEY POINTS

★ Quizzes, downloads, additional support options, bonuses and certificates can add extra perceived value to your course proposition.

★ Consider what job you want each to do – don't just include something for the sake of having it.

★ The exception to this rule is a certificate, which will add considerable value for learners who see it as important to them, but not affect those who aren't fussed about it.

★ Don't let the provision of an 'extra' stop you from getting your course finished and out into the world – you can always add these things in later.

★ Consider the pros and cons of offering extra support before adding this option.

ACTIONS TO GET THAT COURSE ONLINE

☐ Decide whether to include any quizzes in the first version of your course. If you are going to include them, give them a job and be clear on how you will measure their success.

☐ Build your downloadable assets, providing they do not give you a reason to procrastinate from launching.

☐ Think about what (if any) additional level of support or bonuses you want to provide. Set these up and remember to provide appropriate signposts to them and publicity about them.

☐ A completion certificate can often be an effortless way to add lots of extra perceived value, so add one if you can.

Get a handy PDF download of all the chapter summaries and actions at **GetThatCourseOnline.com/Resources**

11

Top tips for getting your recording and filming right first time

CHAPTER ELEVEN

Filming

11

At last! You've got your course planned, your lesson slides created and you are ready to film. You press record and the little red light tells you you're recording and...

Hang on. Whether the thought of recording gives you palpitations (good or bad) or not, there's a bit of information here you might need first. Not least what equipment you need to have and how to set it up. You don't want to fall into the trap of 'all the gear and no idea'...

Tech

You can film your course with nothing more than a smartphone. But the proponents of this method also assume that you are a) comfortable on camera, b) able to talk eloquently about your subject with no mistakes or ums or errs or ahs and c) you are filming everything as a talking head video (see Chapter Nine if this term isn't familiar).

However, if you're following my suggested methodology for your online course, you will need a way to record your screen as well as your voice. There's a way to do this with a smartphone, but honestly, it's much more fiddly and complicated than you need in your life right now.

Similarly with the editing process — which at the very least you will need for trimming the start and finish points of your videos — yes, you could use the freebie editor in YouTube. But it's fiddly and a bit of a blunt instrument. And again, hassle you can easily avoid.

My best suggestion for you is that you invest in something that will do the job of recording you and your slides, gives you a way to edit those recordings and also allows you to either store the videos and link them into your course platform OR gives you the option to produce and download your finished video for storage and upload elsewhere.

I appreciate for those of you new to this stuff, you may have needed to read that last paragraph a couple of times! What you eventually settle on as 'your' method of doing the filming will be dependent on a few other decisions you make along the path of your course creation, so I'm presenting the following as a suitable place to start, but not necessarily the place you'll stay.

Microphone: if you invest in nothing else, please invest in an external microphone rather than using the built-in one on your computer (yes, *any* computer, even your fancy-pants one). Set up properly, this will be far superior to anything built in.

Go for something from Blue like the Yeti or Snowball (I use this), or if you have a little more cash to splash, then a higher spec Rode is a worthwhile investment. You can spend a lot of money on a mic, but generally it's worth it once you know what you're doing. If you're just starting out a Blue Snowball is an excellent choice.

If you need a little more detail to do some more research, go for a 'cardioid' mic. This will help with only picking up the sounds you are making. You could also decide to invest in a headset (after the pandemic you may already have one). This is a viable choice if you are happy with it being on camera with you. Of course, if you have no intention of being on camera ever, that won't matter.

Personally, I don't like a headset if I can help it. For me it feels too much like a call centre, but that is most certainly a personal choice. If you like it, go for it!

You might also want to consider a lapel mic (one that connects to a recording device wirelessly or via a lead) that clips to the front of your clothing. This is only an investment to consider though if you are intending to be standing in front of a video camera (full talking head — and body), instead of recording at your desk.

It works well if you are also using a prop such as a flipchart, as you will naturally turn away from your camera to point to the flipchart or add a note or similar. A stand-alone mic will not consistently capture the volume of your voice with this situation, but a lapel mic will.

A final suggestion to add on to a microphone is to get something called a 'pop filter.' The job of a pop filter is a bit like a screen door that prevents flies and other bugs getting into a house. A pop filter is designed to prevent something called 'plosives' creating an ugly sound in your recording.

Simply put, certain letters in some words are more likely to distort in a recording, which doesn't make for a pleasant listening experience.

Google a pop filter and you'll see what they look like (a stocking over an embroidery hoop!). They are very inexpensive (certainly less than a tenner), but worth buying at the same time as your mic. If you're buying on Amazon, you'll almost certainly be offered one as an additional buying choice. Get it.

Webcam: if budget is tight, use the in-built webcam in your laptop or monitor. If you don't have one, or you would like a better-quality result, then it is worth investing in a webcam. Anything from Logitech would be my go-to. I've used a C920 for years and have no intention of upgrading anytime soon. Like the microphone suggestions, it's a 'plug and play' technology using a USB connection to your computer — Mac users will obviously need an adaptor too.

Software: there are broadly two options to look at here: software that stores videos for you; or software that requires you to download your video for storage elsewhere. Both types give you recording and editing capability. If you want somewhere to record and store your videos in the same place, then look at Loom or Vimeo. Be careful with Vimeo's plans though as you have to be on the Pro plan at minimum to store videos for commercial gain.

If you want to have the ability to store your videos outside of the recording and editing environment, then an excellent budget option is Screencast-O-Matic. Lots of lovely features and a free video editing tool. I know experienced course creators who started with this option and haven't changed.

When you're ready for a few more bells and whistles on the recording and editing front, my go-to is Camtasia from TechSmith. They had a little wobble during the pandemic when an upgrade caused multiple system crashes (I was very grumpy about it), but I reverted to using a previous version until they got it sorted out. Like all tech, there's still an occasional glitch to deal with, but overall it's a great piece of kit.

There are some excellent tutorials provided by Camtasia to help you get started too. It's worth noting that Camtasia is primarily adored by course creators using PCs, even though it does have a Mac version. Mac users tend to gravitate towards Screenflow from Telestream as the equivalent.

You could go all out and invest in something from Adobe. Premier Pro and After Effects will certainly tick the bells and whistles box! I have been trying to find time to develop my skills with these two for a few years now, but it's a steep learning curve and I admit that I run back into Camtasia's arms as soon as I need to produce something quickly.

How do I know if I want separate video storage or not?

It will largely depend on your choice of hosting platform (see the next chapter for this). If you choose a platform that you can upload your videos to, then you may not need to consider storage. If you choose a platform that needs you to provide a link to your videos for 'streaming in', then you will need somewhere for them to be both stored and linked to.

While a hosting solution that you can upload to can be a great initial time and money saver, consider what would happen if that solution were to suddenly become unavailable to you — maybe the service stops, or maybe you are 'locked out' of your account for some reason. It can be a wise move to have your videos stored safely somewhere else.

Videos take up a quite a bit of disk space and if you store your videos on an external hard drive, you cannot stream in from there, so a paid for solution can sometimes be the best option. Generally you will not be able to upload videos directly to your website (a few small ones here and there is often fine, but an entire course isn't usually best practice), so if you're looking at a plugin platform for your course, then you will need a streaming storage service too.

I have separate software for recording/editing and for video storage/streaming.

If you're still not sure whether you will need to have the ability to download your videos or not, read up on the course platform options in the next chapter before making that decision. If you want this decision made first though, choose Loom to get started and then reassess in six months.

Recording/Filming Tips

Let's assume you've got your tech sorted — at least enough to be able to make a start. The next step is to click the 'record' button and away you go. The best way to get better at this stuff is to keep trying, over and over. Even if you are recording most of your course as audio over slides (recommended for the first one), you would be well advised to aim for being on camera at least in the Introduction and Conclusion sections.

This is because in these sections you are trying to inspire your learners to be excited about what's to come and what they're going to learn from you (Introduction); you are also trying to incite them into a specific action such as providing a testimonial and checking out other opportunities to work with you (Conclusion).

Psychology tells us that we are most likely remember the high point and the last point of an experience. The best way to ensure there is a high point is to get learners on board as quickly as possible. Do that by being on camera with a friendly face they can connect with and imagine, while later learning through listening.

The best way to ensure they leave with a great memory of the end point is to be on camera at the end.

By the way, because I adore alliteration (who doesn't?), your middle sections are where you are trying to inform your learners. Inspire — inform — incite: my recipe for online course delivery success.

Here are ten tips in no particular order, to help you get your recording right more quickly than I did:

1. **Camera angle:** please don't force me to look at your nose hair while you're speaking to camera. Put another way, ensure your camera is placed either at, or ideally slightly above your eyeline. Looking down into a camera (usually catches laptop users out) is a terrible angle for the viewer, both aesthetically and psychologically (you are looming 'over' learners on playback which can be unwittingly intimidating).

2 **Look at the camera:** make sure you understand where your camera is so you can look at it. If you feel uncomfortable staring directly at the lens, experiment with the distance you need to be from the camera so you can look slightly above or below it, but it still looks like you're looking directly at it. A little 'dot' sticker or mark of some kind can help you focus (next to, not actually on, the lens obviously).

There are some situations where you can film looking 'off' camera (a bit like a television interview), but for a talking head, looking into camera is best. If you need to imagine you are talking to someone, you could place their picture behind your camera somehow — making sure their eyes are situated close to your camera lens. I know someone who improved their confidence and technique hugely just by placing a stuffed toy bear near their camera. True story!

3 **Sound proofing:** if you don't have your own home studio, then there are a few principles to think about to get the best sound quality possible for your set up. Remember that sound 'bounces' off hard surfaces creating an echo. It is absorbed by soft surfaces. The softer the surfaces around you the better.

If you are in a spacious room with few soft surfaces, you can improve your sound by ensuring your mic is close to your mouth (pro tip: don't speak directly into it, have it slightly to one side of your face).

I've known people who are recording audio over to do so in a cupboard or wardrobe with clothing around them; have a blanket over their screen and their mic (like a sort of children's fort); fashion a 'studio' out of a cardboard box that has only one side open for them to lean into and speak. Have some fun and play around!

Of course, this doesn't work for when you are on camera. Find the best place you can, make sure your mic is close to your mouth and then use the settings in your video editor to play around a bit until you find something that works.

Some people like to use a free software called Audacity to manipulate their sound. I tried this early on in my course creation training, but quickly learnt that there's only so much it can do. It's no substitute for having the best input you can to begin with.

4 **Vocal warm up:** a few minutes spent warming up your vocal cords will cut down the number of silly errors you make. I know it sounds daft, but when I first started recording, I couldn't believe how often I was tripping up over really simple words and phrases. This might not seem like much of an issue, but when it comes to editing, you will thank yourself for not having too many slip ups to edit out.

Your warm-up doesn't have to be anything more taxing than repeating tongue twisters such as 'Unique New York' and 'Red Lorry, Yellow Lorry.' I've even been known to recite the children's song 'Old MacDonald' — noises and all! The point is to ensure that you are using all the muscles around your mouth, so really focus on enunciating every word. A few minutes of this will help save many more minutes of editing, I promise.

5 **Backdrop and clothing:** I confess I spent way longer worrying about this when I first started than I needed to. My very first videos had a bookcase behind me; then I graduated to a colourful shower curtain on a portable clothing rail. Some of my first learners still talk fondly about the shower curtain! After this I had a professional photography back drop, then a plain painted wall for a while, and currently I'm using the photography backdrop again.

I couldn't honestly tell you that my backdrop made a massive difference to the quality of my training. But my theory is that as long as your background isn't too distracting and doesn't contain anything you wouldn't want people to see then you'll be fine. Remember some of the videos from the pandemic where people had clearly neglected to check what 'ornaments' were on their bookcase in the background? Yeah, don't do that... Unless that's your area of expertise of course!

For clothing, I know some experts worry about what they're wearing — do they have to wear the same thing in every video? What if they have their hair styled differently? Please don't spend masses of time worrying about this. It's more important that you feel comfortable, than you feel worried about it.

It's true that wearing an outlandish outfit will cause curiosity in your learners — but maybe this is part of your brand? Apart from that, if you need to go back and redo some videos later, then yes, it's difficult to disguise a big transformation such as long hair to short hair. However, I promise you that aside from a few seconds of noticing a difference, if your content is good, your learners will not make a big deal out of it.

6 **Lighting:** I am not an expert in lighting, but even I know that it's a bad idea to have a window behind you when filming (it casts you into shadow). A good rule of thumb is to make sure that your strongest source of light (which will always be the sun) is in front of you. Many people opt for a ring light to sit behind their camera if they can't film in front of a window with good natural light. I do this and I also use a blackout blind at the window to avoid any lighting changes from clouds etc.

   This can be an issue though if you wear glasses. You may find that there is a reflection from a ring light or even your computer screen when wearing glasses. To counter this, you need to ensure that your strongest light source comes from two places, one either side of you. You could get a couple of angle-poise lamps, or even normal table lamps with strong bulbs and position them on your left and right — experiment with angles as you may be able to effectively use a 45-degree angle to your face.

   Some people have been able to make it work by using an overhead light, or using a photography light reflection panel, so do play around as there are lots of combinations that could work for you. Try your best to avoid having a reflection on your glasses if you can, but as always, don't let this become a procrastination excuse.

7 **Start and end with a smile:** you may have a very pleasing resting face expression (where you are not concentrating on what your face is communicating). I am not so fortunate, and I dare say many people reading this aren't either. You don't want someone's first impression of you to be your resting expression, or you squinting at the screen trying to work out if you're recording or not. Same goes for when you have finished recording — you don't want the lasting impression from the video to be you trying to find the 'stop' button!

   The best way to counter this (and to also give future editing you an easier job) is to start and end each video with a smile. Once you are certain you are recording, or you have finished saying what you need to, stare directly at the camera lens for a couple of seconds with your best full wattage beam. This makes for a much more pleasant beginning and end to your videos for your learners. It also means you are staring at the lens before you start speaking and when you have finished — this is a more professional touch.

There's also the possibility that your video storage platform might take a snapshot of this as the video 'thumbnail' (the picture that shows before the video is played). Of course, you can provide your own thumbnail, but in the interests of speed and ease, having a nice smile makes it happen automatically.

If you're honestly uncomfortable smiling at the camera, or you feel your subject matter isn't compatible with a full wattage smile, please find a friendly expression that you can use, and hold that for a couple of seconds instead.

8 **Clap to break/edit:** when you come to edit your video, you will be able to see a 'track' from the recording that has lots of jagged peaks and deep troughs in it. This is likely the track with your audio on it.

   If you have kept recording during a few takes, or perhaps re-recorded a sentence or two in the middle of a take, an uncomplicated way to see where you have started again is to make a loud noise close to your microphone. You could clap your hands together for example. This will produce an unusually high spike in your audio track, which makes it easy for you to then see where you made a mistake and where you started to correct it. This means you won't have to comb through every video either, unless you want to.

9 **Hold the pose:** if you do make a mistake in the middle of a sentence, try to hold the pose you have with your body and face (if you're on camera) and start your sentence again. This will allow the edit to be as smooth as possible and won't distract your learners.

10 **Break points:** try not to have too many edit points or whizzy effects in your videos unless it's for a specific purpose (maybe you are demonstrating them). As a rule, I will stick to using a fade transition for any edits. I have used other transitions and animations for instances where it enhances what I want to draw attention to, but I use these far less frequently. You don't have to use fade, you might find another transition that you prefer, so just make sure you are consistent with how you treat beginnings, endings and edit points.

A final note on recording and editing: this will 100% guaranteed take longer than you think it will. Allow for this in your planning. I usually tell newbie creators to allow around 30 minutes for every 5 minute video they record — this is for recording and editing once they're up to speed with editing.

Accessibility

It's important to think about accessibility when creating an online course. Lots of people will immediately think about subtitles or captions (there is a difference) when considering this and that's a good start.

Subtitles are shown as the written version of what is being said in a video. For accessibility they should always be white text on a dark background and sentence case. There is a trend towards using different colours and full capitalisation, but this renders the subtitles inaccessible so defeats the point.

Captions go one further than subtitles and include instruction about other noises heard in a video. For example [loud dance music] or [doorbell rings]. These are important to add to allow those who are hard of hearing or deaf to accurately follow everything taking place in a video.

You might be a bit worried that this is starting to sound a bit more complicated than you thought. Remember that if your videos are initially mainly audio over slides, then basic subtitles will be fine.

There are three main ways to get subtitles (which are supplied as an SRT file):

1 You can do them yourself if your editing software has the capability. This can be time consuming and a bit of a learning curve. Frustrating too if your typing skills sometimes go off on a mini-break when you most need them! But this is countered by not costing you anything except your time.

2 You can use an AI system such as Otter.ai, where you will probably have to do some editing to correct errors, but it will still be quicker than doing it all yourself. The system is effectively a 'bot' that is programmed to recognised certain sounds as specific words. You can upload a certain amount for free every month which can be a good help if funds are tight. The yearly plan though is incredibly reasonable and well worth it if you will have a lot of need.

3. You could use a paid service such as Rev.com and pay for a human to provide subtitles, with a much-reduced (but not 0%) incidence of errors creeping in. With a service like Rev.com, you get captions rather than pure subtitles, so this is an added bonus as well as the time saved. You usually pay by the minute of video, so beware of uploading a video that has no voice to transcribe at the beginning.

As well as subtitles or captions, consider providing your learners with an audio file and a transcript of your video lesson too. People like to consume information in diverse ways and this can also aid a deeper learning experience.

For example, I often initially consume a business book through an audio file and if I like what I'm listening to, I will then buy the paperback version to look through and mark up. Sometimes I won't have time to watch a full video, but if there's a transcript, I can skim that for the general idea and come back to the video later.

It is worth seeking out some professional advice in this arena if you know you are likely to be appealing to people with specific needs.

CHAPTER ELEVEN KEY POINTS

- ★ Consider your tech, especially your microphone, webcam and recording/editing software.
- ★ Top tips for recording and filming mean thinking about the senses: how does it look and sound? Think about making life easier for yourself during the editing process. You don't have to wear the same thing every time, but drastic changes in your looks make edits more obvious.
- ★ Recording and editing will take a lot longer than you think.
- ★ Accessibility considerations are fast becoming a 'must have.' Consider the needs of those who struggle to hear or see what you are providing.

ACTIONS TO GET THAT COURSE ONLINE

- ☐ Review your tech and test it out before you start recording for your course. Ask other people what they think about your audio and video quality. Invest if needed (you don't have to spend a fortune).
- ☐ Always warm up your voice before recording to avoid silly mistakes.
- ☐ When on camera, consider your background and what you are wearing, but don't spend ages worrying about this.
- ☐ Make sure you are providing options for those with accessibility needs. Subtitles are the minimum here.

Get a handy PDF download of all the chapter summaries and actions at **GetThatCourseOnline.com/Resources**

12

Everything you need to know about course hosting solutions

CHAPTER TWELVE

Where will my course live?

12

Fair warning: we are about to leap onto the top of one of my favourite soapboxes...

As I briefly mentioned in Chapter Two, there's no such thing as the 'best' anything, when it comes to online course creation. Even if you're reading this book right now thinking "well this is the best book on online course creation" (love you), I guarantee there'll be someone else thinking "meh, it's alright" (it's OK, love you too).

The point is that there's no point in asking what's 'best' — especially when it comes to choosing a hosting platform for your course. There will only be what's right for you, right now. The best thing you can do is be aware of the options and then choose something that suits you for now. Only fossils are set in stone, remember?

So please, don't be that person who goes into a Facebook group on course creation and asks, "What's the best platform for hosting my course?". Guaranteed all you will get is a load of people telling you what they use. How many of them do you think actually took the time to understand what they were doing when they picked? It'll be marginally higher than the number of people who bother to ask you what your situation is before telling you what the 'best' is...

I've even seen some places claim to have conducted a 'true comparison' of the different platforms. It's funny how the top choice for those lists always seems to be the platform the author is using... Affiliate link anyone? (If that last sentence is a mystery, please look up "affiliates" in Chapter Eighteen.)

The other reason it's impossible to provide an answer to the 'best' platform, is that there are so many new ones on the market — with more being added every day. Even software providers that operate in adjacent fields are jumping on the online course provision bandwagon, so this muddies things a little.

Generally, the newer to market, the fewer bells and whistles a platform will have. It's important to consider a few fundamental questions about what you're looking for, so that you can increase your chances of finding the right thing for you first time. More on that in a bit.

> While I'm on my soapbox (I did give you fair warning), if you are digging your heels in about finding the cheapest option or are likely to get sniffy about a platform taking a commission from your course sales, my best advice is to get over yourself!
>
> I'm dead serious. If you want people to pay you for your expertise through an online course, why are you getting all hypocritical and judgey about paying other experts for their expertise to get your course out there? Do you really expect to be able to make money without incurring any costs at all?
>
> If you're feeling stubborn and still thinking "yes I do expect that actually Ginette", please feel free to imagine me shaking my head sadly in your general direction...

I have been through every one of the options I'm about to show you. Not because I can't make up my mind, but because I've been doing this for a long time and needed different things from my platforms at separate times. In fact, as soon as I've finished writing this book, the next project is to review the platforms again for what I need next in my business.

There are broadly four different options available to you for hosting your course, and one of those can also now feasibly be split into three 'sub-options' because of the way the market has panned out. Please note these options are presented for creators looking to sell to individuals — there's a note for other situations at the end of this chapter.

Marketplaces

Dominated by Udemy but there are others that operate in a marketplace style with a slightly different method of assessing payments to instructors. Skillshare is one of these and also LinkedIn Learning (which used to be Lynda.com), but you need to go through an application process for the latter as a recognised expert in your field.

Typically, they will lure instructors in with promises of riches through marketing to their millions of students. The reality is that you will effectively be operating as their marketing department before you get close to seeing any of the numbers they float around. What they market is their platform, using your course among others to attract students in.

Students are 'owned' by the marketplace, with strict rules about how and when you are allowed to communicate with them. You are not allowed to freely promote or invite students 'off platform.' Building an email list of learners will be much harder work than it would be if you were on another type of platform.

If the marketplace promotes your course, it will do so alongside competitor products, often singling out those with higher reviews for special treatment. This leads to extreme gamification of the reviews process (and also makes a mockery of true feedback). There are a minority of instructors who have made a small fortune (and several who will pretend they have).

Typically, the commission rates paid to instructors are low — sometimes as little as 25% of the advertised course price. Affiliates make more and can sometimes 'steal' payments from instructors if the learner happens to have used their affiliate link — even if this was unintentional.

It should be noted that the above is mainly the Udemy model, whereas Skillshare and LinkedIn Learning operate on a 'minutes viewed' system of reward, rather than individual purchase of a course. Udemy also utilises this latter model in their 'Udemy for Business' sub-brand (their competitor product to LinkedIn Learning).

You might now be wondering why on earth anyone would bother with marketplaces. Of all the options, these make it the easiest to create and upload a course. They have excellent walkthroughs, tutorials, knowledge bases and tips. They also serve a vital part of the global market that wouldn't otherwise be able to easily afford some of the training that's on there.

If you're in the market for something that makes it as easy and pain-free as possible, and you don't mind much about your level of compensation for your effort, then it's a very attractive proposition indeed. One thing to be aware of is that when you hit a high enough income threshold, there will be some kind of US-based tax form filling to be done, even if you are not resident of the United States of America.

SaaS Platforms

You may have heard of Teachable and Thinkific in this space. Lots of others, notably Podia and LearnWorlds. They provide Software as a Service (SaaS) — the means to host online courses, including payment gateways if required.

The platform provides a professional look and standard user experience, which (the more you pay them) you can customise to your brand look and feel and even to the point where learners won't realise they are no longer on your main website if that's what you want. You can also use them as your main website too if appropriate.

There is no central library of courses hosted on these platforms (and many instructors don't want this anyway), which means you are entirely responsible for your marketing. SaaS platforms do however manage the admin burden for you very effectively — you will pay commission and there are sometimes payment gateway complications and form filling to be done, but if you are serious about building a following, then these are a good option.

Whichever platform you choose, there will be something that doesn't operate quite as you expected. Go with whichever one feels right to you to begin with, for whatever reason. I initially went with Teachable purely because I didn't like some of Thinkific's early marketing tactics (and Podia or LearnWorlds weren't around then), but otherwise there wasn't a lot to choose between them.

Be aware that there is often quite a bit of change that happens around the free or basic plans offered. If you find a platform you like, invest in the highest appropriate layer as soon as you can, to avoid getting tripped up by a sudden change in what you can do.

There is a slightly different solution to be aware of with the SaaS model, which is platforms that charge per user. Sometimes they also charge per service, per user. One user is a certain price (usually per month billed annually), with things like email, tracking, reporting, quizzing etc. billed as added extras.

Do your research carefully here — while you might not pay much per user initially, the extras add up quickly and unless you are buying on behalf of a client, or have learner numbers in the thousands, you won't see the best cost-per-user price. This may work out to be more expensive than using an 'unlimited learners' platform like those mentioned above.

Plugins

I am concentrating specifically on WordPress plugins here, so if you don't have a WordPress website, this won't apply. If you have a website on something like SquareSpace or Wix, then there are options for you, but they are severely limited. It's the same if you have used a website builder through your website host (such as GoDaddy or 123 Reg).

These options are fine if you only want to have a very basic website. If though, you are at the stage of considering offering online courses through your site, I would strongly urge you to cut your losses now and rebuild on WordPress (you cannot transfer over what you've already built from the other platforms to WordPress).

This is because you will find far greater choice (functionality and cost) on WordPress and it will also be easier to either move your website between hosting providers or change the plugins you choose to use. I should mention I am biased here, as Get That Website Online, providing WordPress hosting and websites, is a business division of mine!

Plugins have developed considerably over the last few years and are now becoming serious contenders with some SaaS platforms. Generally, you will need to be a bit more tech-savvy to get the most out of them (or be working with someone on your website who is).

Key ones to be aware of are LearnDash, LifterLMS or Tutor LMS. Each has pricing options for the best customisation experience and you can create something really on brand and specific to what you want your learners to have. There are various add-on options too but be aware that this can increase the cost quite quickly. Go for something basic to begin with to get your experience underway and then build from there once you have an idea of what else you'd like to offer.

The biggest advantage of using a plugin might also be considered the biggest disadvantage: you have complete control and responsibility for everything. You can make it look and feel the way you want, charge what you want and set whatever rules of engagement you want. You are also responsible for all admin and tech issues (which, when you get into tens, hundreds and even thousands of learners, is quite some undertaking).

Hybrid solutions

These can be split into three — hybrid platforms, hybrid plugins and 'me too' products. They are called hybrid because they offer the ability to not only provide online courses but other functionality too. Generally, they have too much going on for a first-time online course provider — they are also priced at the higher end, so you may find you are paying for things you are simply not ready to use yet.

Hybrid platforms: you will have probably heard of Kajabi and maybe Kartra, New Zenler or FGFunnels in this space. Each offer slightly different additions as well as online courses, but generally they will have the means to hold details of learners, communicate with them and provide something of a membership experience.

Their key selling point is that they allow you to combine all the individual tools you are paying for into one space and one payment as they 'do it all.' Note that even the most well-known and respected (Kajabi) is not perfect and many successful entrepreneurs still prefer to use and pay for additional tools to achieve what they need. This adds extra cost and hassle to something that is supposed to be able to do it all for you in one place.

They can be very effective if the price and functionality is right for you. I would suggest that you need to have offered at least one online course in your business, before you know whether the investment is right for you.

Hybrid plugins: AccessAlly is the front runner here — and personally I love this plugin, the company and everything it strives for. But that's because it suits my business and values. It doesn't mean it would be right for you. Typically, these sort of hybrid plugins offer additional tools just like the hybrid platforms, such as membership-type experiences and links to other automation tools.

My experience is that the hybrid plugins are more agile than hybrid platforms at making changes and adapting to market and user needs, although New Zenler have improved in this area. AccessAlly is certainly an example of this. Again though, these hybrid plugins are only worth the price if you are going to use all or at least most of the functionality.

'Me too' products: these are the platforms and plugins that started life serving a different purpose before adding in functionality to also offer online courses. Think of SamCart (originally a payment gateway and funnel tool), MemberPress (originally a membership plugin) and others.

There is one I know well called GiraffePad, which started life as a tool for trainers to offer a central 'base' for learners attending training and training programmes. Searchie (video search) is another example.

Some of them have done a really decent job of creating an online course experience, but again, think about what you are trying to achieve — if you don't yet use the additional functionality offered, then you probably don't need it yet. These days it's almost more unusual to find a platform or plugin that doesn't claim to offer online course functionality as well.

Think about what you'd like to do and then find the right solution to offer it, rather than the other way around. If you go into research mode without this basic requirement, you will run the risk of being overwhelmed with the possibilities and different marketing pages telling you what you 'must' have.

I have a handy checklist for you of things to think about when comparing where to host your online course. Go to **GetThatCourseOnline.com/Resources** for your copy.

Working with corporate organisations

I promised you a note about this, so here it is. If you are engaged to provide online courses for a corporate organisation, they may well already have their own in-house Learning Management System (LMS). Sometimes they might ask you for recommendations about which one to buy in. If you are not already familiar with the marketplace, I'd politely decline to help with that — it is a huge minefield.

It's important that you find out what system they are using. Some may be big enough to use one of the SCORM-compliant systems that make extensive use of interaction tools (such as Captivate or Artciulate). They may have in-house instructional designers working for them already. Others may use a free open-source software called Moodle.

If SCORM sounds gibberish, please have a look at Chapter Eighteen at the end of this book. If you're not familiar, this will impact your ability to produce something — at least initially until you have the tech skills and software to provide this.

You will either fall into the camp of 'say yes and work it out later' or 'say no and save yourself the embarrassment of not being able to complete the job.' Either way, producing SCORM-compliant courses are not covered in this book because you don't need it to produce your first course or have the additional learning curve that goes with it. That said, the design principles are the same, you just need to be aware of the possibilities available to you with SCORM-compliant software.

The reason you want to find out what system they are using is so you can establish whether you are going to be hosting the online course or they are. If they are, and you have discovered that you don't need to produce a SCORM-compliant solution, then this is quite easy. You make the course, provide the videos and downloads or supporting material. Making it work on their system is up to them. If you have the tech of course, producing SCORM-compliant videos and sending to them is also easy.

If, however, they want you to provide the course hosting, this needs careful consideration as there will be an admin burden on providing both access and tech support, depending on what numbers of learners are being considered. If they want you to host SCORM-compliant videos, be careful here as the platforms that will allow this to happen are often beyond the budget of a small business owner.

This leads naturally into the final part of the corporate 'equation' which is pricing, and is discussed in more depth in the next chapter.

What's this uploading stuff all about?

When you create an online course, you will typically create a lot of videos for learners to follow in a set format. These videos need to be hosted somewhere and displayed in a way that learners can easily see where to start and where to go next.

Some solutions (marketplaces and SaaS platforms) will give you the ability to host your videos with them, so you upload directly to their platform. Usually, plugins will be bound by the rules of the website they're on, which means you will probably want to have a separate place to 'store' your videos, which are then linked to your plugin through your website.

It's not recommended to upload your videos directly to your website, unless you have your own server with massive capacity. If that last bit doesn't mean anything to you, then most likely you don't have it.

Most online course creators will use something like Vimeo, Wistia or Amazon S3 to store their videos. There are other options too — YouTube is the most obvious but doesn't look massively professional when it shows ‘other suggestions’ at the end of your video. You want your learners to go to the next video in your course, not get distracted by cute puppies and kittens!

The place that stores the videos is where you upload them and then you get a video link that you can add to your website. Every time someone watches a video on your website, they are technically watching it being streamed from the video host.

How do I stop my content being stolen?

One thing that concerns new online course creators is the possibility of their content being ‘stolen’ — downloaded and passed around for free. I won’t tell you that this isn’t a possibility, but I will tell you that it’s not worth your worry — at least not yet.

The people who do this sort of thing (steal course content and stream it on a ‘torrent’ site) usually only target the very successful courses and programmes — the people making more than six or seven figures a year from their content. But those people are also making enough money in the first place to employ services to spot and stop these things happening.

Think of it as a cost of doing business. You don’t want to ignore it completely, but you also don’t want to spend all your time trying to beat the hackers. Much better to spend your time creating and optimising for the people who are your real audience — the ones who will happily pay you for the great content you provide. Remember the Online Course Taker’s Mantra: *“At an appropriate price for the value delivered.”*

There’s another reason not to worry about this too: knowledge doesn’t equate to action. Take this book for example. You have purchased the entire methodology and knowledge you need to create an online course. But that doesn’t mean a thing if you don’t put any of this knowledge into action. In other words, you won’t be able to take advantage of my generosity in giving you all this knowledge for an incredibly low investment, if you don’t do anything with it.

I anticipate there are broadly three types of people who will be consuming this book:

1. Genuine experts who want to learn and put this stuff into action. Whether you do this or not depends on more than just purchasing this book.

2. Course creation trainers who want to check out the competition and perhaps enhance their offering if I've mentioned something they think they've missed. Or of course, feel very smug if they think they know something that I have missed. Entirely possible!

3. Wannabe course creation trainers who want to take my knowledge and pass it off as their own.

Guess who I've written this book for? Yep, it's the first group. Just because there's a possibility that the second and third group might do what I've suggested, it isn't a good enough reason for me to not write the book. After all, with the second group, I couldn't say that I haven't learnt anything from other course creation trainers.

Although I've never taken a specific programme from anyone who is a course creation trainer, I've taken other programmes that contain some information about course creation and I've certainly availed myself of freebies being offered. If it helps more people be able to provide great online courses instead of the barrage of rubbish that's (also) out there, this can only be a good thing as far as I'm concerned.

The only bits that I will consider taking any action over are the Mantras at the beginning of this book. They are 100% my creation and I can prove it! Everything else is information I have learned along the way in my own journey of discovering what does and doesn't work. As long as someone isn't using my words and content verbatim, then I don't have an issue with the methodology being mirrored — it would be quite difficult to create an effective and engaging course without most of the steps I've already covered.

The point is that people who are only interested in getting something for free — illegally or otherwise — usually aren't the people who would ever consider buying your course in the first place. They're not your target audience. And just because they have the information, it doesn't mean they will do anything with it. There's plenty of research out there that shows we don't place the same perceived value on free stuff as much as the stuff we pay for.

My best advice is therefore to stop worrying about your content being stolen as quickly as you can — concentrate on providing a wonderful experience for the people who do value and respect your knowledge and time. You'll be much happier!

CHAPTER TWELVE KEY POINTS

- ★ There's no such thing as the 'best' platform to host your online course, only something that's right for you, right now.
- ★ There are four main options to choose from: marketplaces, SaaS platforms, plugins and hybrid solutions.
- ★ Depending on your chosen solution, you may need to have somewhere to store your videos too.
- ★ Worrying about protecting your content from being stolen isn't the best use of your time. Create for the people who will value and respect your time instead.

ACTIONS TO GET THAT COURSE ONLINE

- ☐ Consider what will suit you right now for hosting your course. Do you just want to get it out there, or do you want greater control over your marketing and earning options?
- ☐ Download my guide about things to consider when choosing a platform from **GetThatCourseOnline.com/Resources**
- ☐ Make your platform decision and move on. You can always change later down the line when you have more experience.

Get a handy PDF download of all the chapter summaries and actions at **GetThatCourseOnline.com/Resources**

13

Three important truths when it comes to pricing your online course

CHAPTER THIRTEEN

What should I charge?

13

I'm willing to bet that there are a fair number of people who have got hold of this book, checked the chapter titles and come straight to this page.

Are you rumbled?!

If it is true for you or not, there's something about pricing online courses that gets people all kinds of concerned. I'd be lying if I said that wasn't me too in the early days of learning this stuff. I can virtually guarantee that you will also price 'incorrectly' to begin with — but treat this as the learning point it is and you'll be fine.

So let me begin by telling you three important truths when it comes to pricing your online course:

1. There is NO formula for this. Seriously. You may as well pick a number, multiply it by orange and subtract toast — you'll have more of an idea about pricing than most.
2. The price of your course has NOTHING to do with the length of your course. Zip. Zilch. Nada. This is troublesome sometimes for experts who are used to pricing based on an hourly or daily rate.
3. The price is ALWAYS less important than you think for the person who is in the right place (looking for the solution you offer) to benefit from your expert help.

Well, there we are then. All you need to know about pricing your online course. No? Oh alright then...

While you really could pick a number out of thin air and call that the price of your course, most people feel more comfortable having a rule of thumb to follow. In the absence of finding a good guide, you might also conduct some research on the internet.

Sooner or later, you end up on Udemy and have that heart-sinking moment where you see tens, if not hundreds of courses being offered on your specialist subject for less than a decent bottle of wine. Ugh.

I really need you to absorb this next message: unless you are placing your course on Udemy (see the previous chapter for my thoughts on that), you do not have to compete with them on price. I promise.

Not long after that, if it hasn't happened already, the sneaky little mind-fart that says "Why would anybody pay for this when it's available for free on YouTube?", may also try to stink up your mojo. Don't listen!

You think a Michelin-starred restaurant cares about a 99¢ cheeseburger from a fast-food joint? After all, they're both providing food, aren't they? Of course they don't care! Firstly because they know their regular customers are unlikely to be fast-food afficionados and secondly because they know they are technically selling the same thing but the point is that they are doing it differently. They provide a differentiation of quality and service. And possibly other areas too.

This is how you should think about your pricing. Maybe you aren't creating a Michelin-equivalent, but what you are doing is creating something different to anything else out there. The difference is you. How you approach the subject, explain the concepts and help people understand. You aren't trying to help everyone possible, just those who connect with the way you do it. And there will be people that value your style above anyone else's. You just need to create a way for them to easily find you.

Think about your price as a function of the value you deliver. Will your course help someone to earn more? Then that needs considering in your price. Are you offering lots of additional support with the course? Then that also needs taking into account. Maybe you are looking at selling into corporate organisations, rather than to individuals. Again, that will be something to think about for your pricing model.

You may also want to consider where your course 'sits' in your overall business strategy. This, though, is a more advanced process than the intended level of this book, so I won't go into too much detail here. Just know that pricing when using your course strategically, rather than as a stand-alone product you offer, is different. Get in touch to find out how I can help you with that.

Online courses work well as part of a blended learning package, as pre-training and refresher options for example. In this case the pricing model is more about the overall programme than the individual course.

For the remainder of this chapter, I will talk you through how to think about your pricing for selling single courses to individuals and how to think about your pricing for selling into corporate organisations.

Selling to individuals

Ignoring Udemy, there will probably be a modal point of pricing in your area of expertise. If you can find this point, then you have a choice. You can either use your pricing to place your course as a direct competitor or you can deliberately price vastly lower or higher.

If you want to be seen as a direct competitor, then you will need to also concentrate more of your marketing on what differentiates you from your competitor courses. Do you offer better bonuses, a quicker or easier path to results perhaps?

Maybe you want to undercut the competition to gain market share as quickly as possible — perhaps to later sell on additional courses or other ways of working with you. Be careful though — there will be a point where buyers will think your offer is too good to be true. For example, if your competitors are all around the $497 point and you offer the 'same' content for $4.97, there's going to be some cynicism about the real value you offer. You'd better make sure you have several amazing and authentic testimonials to back you up.

You could decide to go high — much higher than your competitors. Perhaps you feel that your methodology is vastly superior and you can prove it. Perhaps you have an incredibly strong brand and loyal following.

And if you think this strategy couldn't possibly work, think about the price of the latest iPhone compared to the leading Android smartphone.

Most people though, when new to offering online courses, want to ensure their pricing is 'as expected.' This is the quickest and easiest solution until you are more experienced at online business. I'm not going to attempt to talk you out of this.

If you can't find a modal pricing point though, consider the following as a rule of thumb to start you off and remember to err on the side of higher rather than lower. This is not so you can discount, as many would say, but because most people underestimate the value they are providing.

A quick note on pricing psychology. Rage against it if you want, but it has been proven time and again that 'charm' pricing — using a seven or a nine at the end of a price — makes a difference. This is why you'll see so many courses priced at $97, $497, $997. Logically we know that this effectively means $100, $500 and $1,000. But emotionally we don't weigh it up that way.

If you're so special that pricing psychology doesn't apply to you, go for it. The rest of us might half listen to you bemoaning your lack of sales while we're counting our bank balance...

OK, now that's dealt with, here's how to think about your price:

If you are offering a course that gives people a small part of the journey to expert-level understanding, then your course is probably around the $97 mark. If it's a bigger chunk of the journey (say a quarter or a half), then it's probably around $497. If you're offering the whole journey — a big transformation, or chunk of learning that enables them to 'level up' in some way, then you're looking at the $997 and beyond mark.

Working out the price:

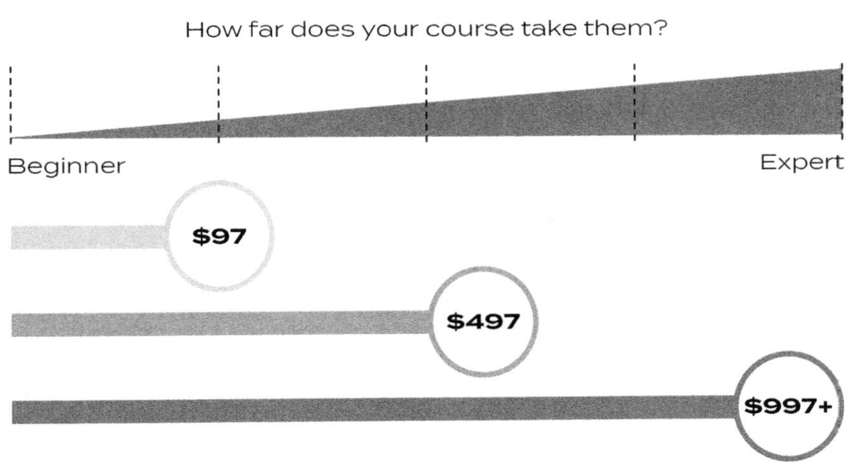

By the way, you can also go beyond $997 if you want, but you will need to think about your offer and your marketing slightly differently. For a first online course, I'd stick to getting something smaller completed. Remember this is initially about learning the skill of online course creation, rather than necessarily creating a 'flagship' product.

After all this, just pick a price. Make the decision, move on. Don't let it become a point of procrastination!

Selling to corporate organisations

A trainer friend of mine says that the rate you should ask for is as much as you can say without laughing. This might seem flippant, maybe even open to abuse, but the reality is that many individuals struggle to price themselves appropriately, especially for the corporate market.

Another trainer friend of mine emphasises the need to be crystal clear on what your training can deliver to the organisation in terms of the bottom line. How much money will it save them if they implement your recommendations?

Either of these approaches will give you a starting number. After that, you have to go with what feels right. While there is no formula for this, I have developed an approach which helps clients get started with a number, which they can then manipulate as they see fit.

This works if you already have a day-rate that you sell into corporate organisations for training delivery. Simply work out the cost per head of your in-person delivery and then price your online course at around 75% of that. Make sure you use these numbers in your proposal so the client sees they are getting a 'reduced' cost per head number. You can also bring the percentage per head down (never below 50% unless you are talking about thousands of people) for increased numbers.

Although you could choose to offer a per person proposal (so if they only want 8, they only pay for 8), I advise saying the price point is 'up to' a certain number — if they end up using fewer than the amount they have bought that's up to them.

Let's use a fictional example to illustrate this. Imagine we have created the Perfect Toast course of earlier chapters. We have already developed a good working relationship with the National Catering College, which happens to be in our town. We've delivered a few in-person training days there for $1,200 a day for 10 trainee chefs.

The College has realised that they have a deplorable lack of basic skills in perfect toast-making, so have asked for the Perfect Toast online course to be supplied. We know that our in-person per person day rate is $120 ($1,200 divided by 10 trainee chefs).

Our proposal contains the following table to help the College see how much it would cost to put different numbers of people through our online course:

Number of people	Percentage of per person day rate (%)	Cost per person ($)	Fee ($)	In-person fee ($)
Up to 10	75	90	900	1,200
Up to 20	70	84	1,680	2,400
Up to 35	60	72	2,520	4,800
50+	50	60	3,000	6,000+

There are other things you can consider such as a licensing model, where you allow access for a certain number of people for a certain period of time. Bear in mind though that if you are providing the material for them to host on their systems, you don't really have the ability to check if they are abusing this — or indeed the number of people having access to the course.

What a licensing model will do though, is give you a reason to get back in touch after a year or so, with a license renewal invoice or maybe an 'updated' version of your course (make sure there really are updates in there) if applicable. It's a great business model.

"Now wait just a minute there Ginette," you say, "you told me categorically that price has nothing to do with length, but now we're working out a price based on a day rate!"

Yeah. Rumbled. My only excuse here is that you needed something to give you a way to come up with an initial figure. If you have a per person day rate, it's a start. And your course is unlikely to be the equivalent of a day in length (8 hours of video? No thank you — we work to the Online Course Taker's Mantra!).

Remember that you should consider the value of the course transformation first and foremost. If the numbers spitting out from these calculations don't feel right, pick another number.

But what if you don't have a handy day rate? Well now we're back into the realms of making one up. Think back to what I was saying about the level of transformation — if you're delivering up to say 20% of the journey to expert level, then it's around $100 per person (which can be reduced as per the previous table).

Ultimately there are other factors to take into consideration and you should try to get an idea of their budget if you can, to make sure you are not wildly out of their range. This is often easier said than done of course, but someone has to blink first. At least if you offer an opening number that you would be more than happy with, you are able to pitch the opening negotiation point.

What currency should I use?

If you are selling to your home market only, then use your home currency. Be aware that the cheaper course hosting platforms often only allow you to have one currency though. And the internationally accepted currency for online courses is US Dollars. Great for those of you in the States, not always such a great thing for anyone outside.

Selling to a global audience is one of the fantastic and frustrating things about providing online courses. It's fantastic because it opens up a larger market for you. It's frustrating because of the different tax rules. In the UK, Brexit has caused all sorts of fun and games here when selling back into the EU. Although, to be fair, it wasn't massively easy to work out before that...

All I can say to you is to get professional advice. And by professional advice I do not mean random internet people. Especially the ones in social media groups that are busy telling everyone how to run their business with no proof of expertise, let alone professional indemnity insurance.

A qualified professional will at least have standards they need to reach and a professional body you can turn to if they do you wrong. Who do you complain to when Fred off the internet told you something that you didn't bother to check? But hey, if you're happy to place your business in a stranger's hands, that's up to you...

How do I stop refunds?

You can't and you shouldn't. Yes, I'm aware there are all sorts of courses and well-known course providers out there with all sorts of interesting stipulations about what you have to provide and 'prove' just to receive a refund.

Generally, I'm not a massive fan of 'shoulds' and 'shouldn'ts' but in this instance I'm going to use them. You *should* give a refund if someone asks for one and you *shouldn't* waste your energy trying to fight it.

Here's why: most people are intrinsically good. If they sign up to your course, they will do so with the intention of completing the course. But then life happens. Maybe it's buyer's remorse, maybe their cat got run over. Maybe they were feeling flush and decided they'd find a way to make the payments, even though they didn't know how. And then couldn't.

There are all sorts of reasons that people have for requesting a refund. And honestly, I can't be bothered to think of them all and then fight them. I have better things to do with my time. What I tend to do is make sure that there are some basic things in place to deter people from consuming my stuff and then trying to get their money back.

First up I make sure there is a guarantee on the sales page and in the course terms and conditions (see the next chapter) that says refunds will be granted without question within the first 14 days of purchase. I'm happy to keep hold of their money for that period before I allocate it elsewhere in the business.

I will make sure that if there are downloads included with the purchase, the terms state that the legal 14-day cooling-off period that applies in my country is waived if items are downloaded before 14 days are up. Check what the legalities are in your country.

Realistically though I will usually always grant a refund in the first 14 days because the person's access to the course materials and any groups will be removed if they refund. Simple. Could someone still abuse this? Yes. Am I going to waste my energy on the minority of muppets that do these things? Nope. Karma will sort that one out for me.

After 14 days, I always take it on a case-by-case basis. It will vary depending on the terms I've offered at sign up — payment plans for example can make things muddy, but I will always try to play fair by the person and by me.

Secondly, I will make sure there is something offered with the course that can be taken away in the event of a refund. It might be access to a Facebook group, access to the course, removal from something else. It doesn't really matter what, the point is that there has to be a clear idea of what is lost if a refund is requested. If someone doesn't feel a potential sense of loss, there's no incentive not to request a refund.

Refunds are a cost of doing business. You won't be able to avoid them, so just make sure you are spending as little time as possible worrying about them. Of course, if you're getting more refunds than people staying, there's something drastically wrong somewhere, so work that out quickly!

But I don't do Facebook

If, as I've suggested in Chapter Ten, you provide some sort of community for your learners, you may get one or two people angling for a discount because "I don't do Facebook". Be noticeably clear in your terms, that being on Facebook (or wherever) is not mandatory to see course success. There's no reason to give them a discount if they choose not to join in. The price is the price for the course — anything else is a bonus.

Charging for my content is tricky because...

Offering a course for free as part of a lead generation strategy is valid and can be very effective. But occasionally I come across experts who struggle with the idea of charging appropriately (or even anything at all) for their course because of community culture.

Specifically, the notion that if your area of expertise, or 'gift' is concerned with helping people get out of a difficult or troubling life situation, you should give it away for free. I see this all the time with the more creative and empathetic professions. There is a misconception that if you are helping humanity, somehow you shouldn't need to be paid for it.

I call BS. This is NOT a good enough reason for you to not charge appropriately. What it is doing is exposing the money mindset blocks in your community and you. Find a good money mindset mentor that you feel a connection with (my favourites are Denise Duffield Thomas and Jen Sincero, but there are many) and work on that stuff until you feel strong enough to stand up for your right to earn money doing something that also helps humankind. There are far too many people in the world who get rewarded for ultimately hurting humanity. Isn't it time to redress the balance?

Should I offer a pricing plan?

If you are offering a course at the higher end of the pricing we've discussed, then you can offer a pricing plan if your hosting solution allows (most will). Don't offer it for the lower end — if someone can't afford $97 in one hit, then they are likely to default or refund anyway. Also, they are most likely going to find what they want on Udemy. Not your customer in the first place.

There are two ways of offering a pricing plan: people paying in full get the cheapest rate and those paying on a pricing plan end up paying more for the same thing OR you simply divide the total cost by however long the plan is for (2–12 months) and that's what they pay. I would advise going with the former as with pricing plans there is higher risk to you of defaulting payments. There's certainly a higher admin burden too.

Remember though, you don't have to do this. Often you will see it offered by those who can afford to take the risk. If you can't, then don't!

CHAPTER THIRTEEN KEY POINTS

★ There's no formula for pricing your course. Seriously. Everyone just makes it up.

★ Your price should be linked to the level of transformation you offer, not the length of time it takes to consume your content.

★ If selling to individuals, stick to the expected norms with your competition to begin with. You'll soon work out if it's priced appropriately or not. Be prepared to get it wrong to begin with.

★ If selling to corporate organisations, work out a per head rate and think about bulk discounts.

★ Price in USD for a global audience, and always take professional advice on the tax situation for you.

★ Always allow refunds to happen with the least negative energy you can spare.

★ Don't offer discounts because someone chooses not to do something that's included in your course.

★ Pricing plans work for higher priced courses, but you don't have to offer them.

ACTIONS TO GET THAT COURSE ONLINE

- [ ] Pick a price and go with it. Use the information in this chapter as a starting point.
- [ ] Sort out your money mindset issues! You deserve to be paid appropriately for your expertise.

Get a handy PDF download of all the chapter summaries and actions at **GetThatCourseOnline.com/Resources**

14

How to avoid the biggest problem I see with most online course sales pages

CHAPTER FOURTEEN

Writing the sales page

14

If you've put in the work to properly understand your audience, as outlined in earlier chapters (Three, Four and Five if you need a little nudge here), then this bit will be a breeze. The biggest problem I see with most online course sales pages is that they concentrate way too much on *what* learners will get, but nowhere near enough on *why* those things are important and should be valued.

Even a cursory glance at the internet will find you no end of promises offering 'the' sales page formula. There's no doubt this is a highly skilled and sought-after area of expertise. But you may not have the funds or contacts to find the right copywriter for you initially. If you have a good understanding of your audience though, you can write your own sales page — at least until you've made enough money to employ a specialist.

You might wonder how you're going to make that money if you haven't got an amazing sales page to begin with. Here's the thing: your sales page is only responsible for about 20% of your marketing. I do not have any official statistical evidence to back this up, other than my own experience and that of my clients. Believe me or don't, it won't change what you need to do, but it might change your level of success!

If you think that having a killer sales page is going to do all the marketing work for you, then my friend you are in for a rude awakening. Yes, it's important to have some key bits on there — most noticeably asking for the sale and providing a means for potential learners to sign up.

But the role of a sales page is more to function as the final convincer, not the whole funnel. For a more detailed explanation of funnels, have a look in Chapter Eighteen at the back of this book.

This isn't true for sales pages for all products. But for online courses you would have to be extremely lucky (and probably closely related to the world's top copywriters) to have a sales page that successfully acted as introducer, nurturer and convincer all in one.

So what's the point of the sales page then? Well, it needs to contain the information a potential learner is both expecting to find (what's this thing all about, and how much is it) and needs to have (why it's the right choice for them, how to pay), so that it 'seals the deal' of the course promise.

Think about it like this: I have made you several promises in this book, but until you are convinced of my words, those promises aren't going to work on their own. If they did, I could just write a book that said, 'Do this, then that, it'll work, I promise' and you'd be convinced and everyone's a winner. Actually, hang on...

> Before I go too much further, I should cover off something that had me mightily perplexed in the early days of my online course creation learning: what's the difference between a sales page and a landing page? There's more explanation in Chapter Eighteen, but for now, as far as you need to know to get your course online, you can think of them as the same thing.
>
> The only reason I am including this little tangent is that I have been on platforms where the two terms are used interchangeably, which was initially worrying, then annoying, then something I ceased to care about. Although there is a difference between the two types of page you don't need to be side-tracked with that bit of knowledge yet.

Back to our sales page. I mentioned the information a learner is both expecting to find, and needs to have, on a sales page. This information serves to underline some of what they have already gone through: finding out about you, your course and feeling connected and curious enough to want to view the course sales page. It also provides the next step of knowledge they need to convince themselves that the course is right for them.

Wait, what? Convince *themselves*?

Yep. Here's something, that to my mind, isn't talked about enough when it comes to ethical marketing persuasion: we don't manipulate anyone into doing anything; we simply provide the triggers for them to persuade themselves.

Sure, there are some shady people out there who abuse the sometimes very powerful triggers available, to manipulate someone into thinking a particular course of action is right for them. I'm not talking about those people or those choices. I certainly won't be advising you to do anything that isn't ethically sound. Assuming your ethics align with mine of course...

There are fundamentals to constructing a good sales page. We need to present information that helps the reader — helps them form the internal arguments they need to answer an emphatic 'Yes!' to the following key questions:

A Is this something that can help me to either get rid of a pain or achieve a goal?

B Do I believe it will work for me?

C Do I relate to and trust the person I will be learning from?

D Does the price in relation to the value reassure me that this is at the level and quality I am looking for?

And while we need to help them answer those key questions, the way in which we do that needs to be tailored to their starting point, the language they use around the subject and of course the common barriers or obstacles they perceive that have stopped them so far.

Shortly, I will give you the outline structure of a simple sales page. There are lots of variations you could have and you could probably see dozens of examples of sales pages on the internet and find variations on this structure. I have training available in more advanced sales page structures, but I don't want to overcomplicate this for you right now. You need to start somewhere and this is my recommendation.

Also, don't try to wordsmith your page immediately. Don't try to get the phrasing or the tone exactly right. Get the basic blocks into place and then work out the exact copy (words) later. If you try to wordsmith as you go, you will end up in a spiral of perfectionism — trust me, I've been there!

Features and benefits

Lots of people get a bit excited over features and benefits and how you should only use benefits on your sales page. This is incorrect.

You need both features and benefits, but you need to introduce them in a particular order. This is because of the way we process information and reason with ourselves about making a purchase. There's lots of psychology behind this (see **GetThatCourseOnline.com/Resources** for more), but simply put, we need to have the emotional information (benefits) first and then the logical information (features) second. Both are designed to set expectations for what the learner will get.

Features are generally the tangible aspects of an offer such as the number of videos, the downloads, the amount of time it will take to complete the course. You could describe features as being the bits someone can see or hear when taking your course.

Benefits are the more intangible outcomes of the offer. They can speak to the emotional upside of the new knowledge that will be received. You could describe the benefits as being the bits someone feels when taking your course. They might also be described as the outcome, but it's deeper than just having a new skill.

It sounds easy to distinguish when described like that, but sometimes it can be a bit less clear. If you're stuck on the distinction for a particular aspect you want to describe on the sales page, use this little trick:

Write down or think about the aspect and then follow it with the statement 'Which means that'. For example:

FEATURE		BENEFIT
Bite-sized videos that can be watched at your leisure	**Which means that**	You'll no longer feel frustrated at having to find a whole block of free time to take the course
Conveniently fit the course around your other commitments	**Which means that**	It's easy and stress-free to level up your knowledge

If 'which means that' isn't working, you can also try asking yourself "why is this important?" until you can't think of any other reasons. There's also the more blunt "so what?" that I occasionally wheel out too — usually to emphasise that this is about what will make a difference to the learner, not what the course creator thinks is important.

Simple sales page structure

From top to bottom, here are the 14 blocks you need, along with the key question they directly relate to. You will see that all the key questions (referenced by using A, B, C, D) are covered between four and five times:

A Is this something that can help me to either get rid of a pain or achieve a goal?

B Do I believe it will work for me?

C Do I relate to and trust the person I will be learning from?

D Does the price in relation to the value reassure me that this is at the level and quality I am looking for?

1. **Your hook:** this is your course title and promise **(A)**

   There's a lot of stuff to learn around creating a great hook, but the most important bit to understand is that you want to help someone decide straight away whether it is worth their while reading on. If you have got your title and your promise right by following the steps I showed you in Chapter Five, then you've got this covered.

2. **The villain:** the biggest obstacle they perceive is in their way **(A, C)**

   Even if you have already covered this off in your promise, this is where you elaborate on the biggest obstacle you've identified they have. You need a paragraph or two to describe the situation or issue they most likely face. The idea is to have them nodding in agreement as if to say: "Yes, that's what it's like!". Put it into a little story that they can imagine themselves in, if you can.

3. **Why now:** why now is the ideal time to do something about the issue **(A)**

   Here you are helping them to see that action is the only antidote to the obstacle. If there is genuine urgency (an industry deadline, an upcoming national holiday, year-end etc.) you can use this. If there is not genuine urgency, then you need to help them see that continuing as they are, is unlikely to get them far. Again, this can be no more than a couple of paragraphs.

4 **Credibility:** why you are the person to help them **(C)**

You don't need a full biography here. What you are trying to do is make yourself relatable to the person reading your sales page. Talk about your experience as it relates to them — have you been in their shoes, how do you know what obstacles they're facing? You can list your qualifications if it's relevant and a clear authority marker in your area of expertise. Try to tell a story of how you made a breakthrough in understanding. Don't just list your CV.

5 **Future-pace:** what life will be like after they've taken your course **(B)**

Here you are bringing them a verbal picture of how much better their situation will be once they have the knowledge you are promising in your course. Another couple of paragraphs will work and if you're stuck for a beginning, use this: 'Picture this:...' and go on to describe a scenario where the obstacles have been obliterated and life is wonderful.

6 **Offer intro:** first introduction of what they get, plus any bonuses offered **(D)**

In this block you are going heavy on the benefits — this doesn't mean you can't list the features, but don't go all in on listing everything. This is the introduction to the offer, so you want to concentrate on the emotional benefits of taking the course rather than the full list of features of the offer. Tell them it's a video course, tell them about the downloads, tell them about your bonuses but always with the explanation of why those things are great news for them.

7 **Price intro:** the investment, any equivalence **(D)**

This is where you list the price of your course and where you help them put that price into a context. For example, you may equate the price of your course to buying a piece of equipment they might commonly use, or something else they would buy without questioning the cost.

Often you will see prices broken down into a daily, weekly or monthly cost and the equivalence of that. Be careful comparing the daily cost to a cup of coffee though — this one is heavily over-used.

If you have any payment plans, list them too and also list out your bonuses, with a value price attached to each. If you do have bonuses, be sure to calculate the full price of the course plus bonuses to point out how much value they are getting for a small investment. And yes, using 'investment' instead of 'price' or 'cost' is a good idea too.

Don't forget that this is where your button or link to make payment goes.

8 **FAQs:** frequently asked questions **(B, C)**

It would be more accurate to say this block is about 'frequently encountered objections to being able to sort out the issue'. Here you are trying to list out as many objections you can think of that your potential learner will have as to why the course won't work for them. You should have this already from the exercise at the end of Chapter Three.

The FAQs are there for you to counter those objections and to be clear about what the course can (and can't) do for someone. Typical FAQs include any sentence starting with 'But what if?'

Also, somewhat counter-intuitively, it can help to include one that says 'no, this course can't do that' — this shows integrity. You could use this one as a joke too: "But what if there's a zombie attack while I'm watching the videos?" "Well, in that instance, please apply for a refund to HelpZombiesHaveAttacked@mycourse.com and we'll see what we can do".

Actually, I quite like that example. Head to **GetThatCourseOnline.com/Course** and you might see it in the FAQs...

9 **Social proof:** any case studies or testimonials **(B, C)**

If you have evidence that proves your methodology or training has worked, this is where you include it. If you don't have anything specific to your course or related training you have done, include any general testimonials you have for now. If you don't have any of those, ask for some! Go to your LinkedIn contacts, your network, your colleagues — anyone who you think might be willing to provide a paragraph for you. Testimonials work best if they are about the breakthrough someone has had because of your teaching, rather than general praise of how wonderful a human being you are — which I'm sure you are, but as a testimonial these are less effective.

If you can, include different mediums too. A mix of straightforward quotations, screenshots of praise on social media and short videos from real learners works well. As a guideline, you are looking to include at least ten if you can. Some sales pages go over the top with these — try not to put people in an endless scroll of testimonials that get tedious to go through!

10 **Solution comparison:** what other options are available to them **(D)**

If you completed the actions in Chapter Four, you should already have a fairly good understanding of what other options are available for your potential learners to solve their problem or achieve their goal. In this block, you are going to provide a ready-made comparison of those options, which naturally paints the option of taking your course in the most promising light.

This takes advantage of the truth that human beings are excellent at finding shortcuts to understanding. If someone has already done the research for us, why repeat it? So take advantage of this natural situation by providing the comparison that makes your course seem like a no-brainer.

List out the features and benefits of your course and then compare how the other solutions stack up. You are looking for a table that shows ticks against everything for your course and not so many ticks against the other solutions. As long as your features and benefits are plausible, and your comparison of those are honest, this works really well.

Here's an example of what you can see on the sales page for our Perfect Toast course (**GetThatCourseOnline.com/Toast**):

	How to Make Perfect Toast online course	**Toast Makers' Membership**	**Toastally Awesome Snacks recipe book**
Video training	✓		
Step-by-step instructions	✓		✓
Facebook group	✓	✓	✓
Instructor support	✓	✓	
Money-back guarantee	✓	✓	

11 **Dream state:** the hidden aspirations they have **(A, B)**

This one can sometimes be a little more elusive for newbie online course creators not used to thinking about this stuff. You may have heard of this being referred to as 'the benefits behind the benefits.' What this means is that there is often a 'hidden' desire behind wanting to achieve the solution to a pain or reach a particular goal. And this desire is usually connected to ego or perceived social status within a peer group.

For example, your course may help someone to be better at their job, maybe even get a pay rise or a promotion. The 'hidden' desire behind this is usually one of status uplift — being thought of as higher in social status because they have achieved these things.

If you can accurately identify what the hidden desire might be for your potential learners and you can write a paragraph about it that feels authentic but not sleazy or creepy, then include it here. Remember you are trying to present yourself as a trusted and credible source to learn from, not a judgemental relative or spammy hacker claiming to have access to their webcam!

12 **Offer repeat:** repeat the offer **(D)**

Repeat the offer block, but this time list out all of the features and benefits of the offer. Your aim here is to give all the details of everything they will get by paying you money. You are setting expectations of what they'll get and what they'll need to do to achieve it (how long, how often, pre-work, homework etc.).

13 **Price repeat:** repeat the investment **(D)**

This is a repeat of the pricing block, but without the full equivalence information. You could refer to anything you have previously used in your rationalisation such as 'remember this is the equivalent of X', but you don't need the full explanation. Remember to include the pay button or link again.

14 **Guarantee:** making it a no-lose, no-brainer decision **(B, C)**

One of the reasons people end up not buying is often more to do with fear over loss. If they buy your course and it doesn't work, they might lose their money, their time, they might even lose face with people in their circle who were cynical about the investment in the first place.

Your final block of the sales page is designed to reassure people that this is a no-lose investment for them. The most common way to do this is by using a money-back guarantee. Remember in Chapter Thirteen I talked about refunds? This is where the broad details of your refund conditions sit. The full detail sits in your Terms and Conditions, discussed shortly.

If you can, try to paint a positive picture to go alongside those conditions, showing confidence in your course's ability to deliver the promise. For example:

"I'm confident that you will be able to immediately take advantage and see the benefits of what I show you before you've even finished the course. But I also understand that sometimes life gets in the way of what we want to do, so if you need to get your money back within 14 days of purchase, I will send it back with no questions asked, guaranteed."

What about images and videos?

Here's another area that can provide plenty of fertile ground for procrastination. It's quite possible to spend (waste) days on trying to find the right images for your sales page. Please don't fall into this trap. There are some sales pages that have no images at all, but that's a topic for another time.

Just try to find images that are free to use or pay for a license to use images from a stock provider. I talked about this in Chapter Nine. Beyond that, if they look like they are relevant to your course topic, then great.

I would advise having around four or five images on your sales page. One for the header or 'hero' image, with your course title and promise over the top. The rest spread evenly over the page to break up the text. It's also a sensible idea to have some form of 100% guarantee image for your final block too.

Yes, there is more to learn here and there's also some stuff to think about around your branding too BUT all of this can be worked on later. You don't need to have this stuff nailed for your first one. Just pick what you like and you think would not offend your potential learners. Beyond that it's incremental improvements that can be made and you have time after launch, I promise.

If you are comfortable to do it, having a video at the top of your sales page, where you are on camera talking through the various blocks on your sales page, that's great. But please know that this is not necessary for your first course. This is something you can work up to as you get more confident doing these things. Plus, there are different sorts of videos you can make in your promotional efforts, which I talk about in the next few chapters.

Terms and conditions

I would strongly recommend that you have a set of terms and conditions attached to the order page (also known as the checkout page). Most platforms will have this ability built in, you just have to provide the terms and conditions — or occasionally fill in the relevant blanks. Seek legal advice for something that will hold up in a court of wherever your jurisdiction is. Make sure you specify which jurisdiction that is, so you don't find yourself subject to action in a foreign country.

You want to cover off the usual things such as access rights, copyrights, payment terms, income disclaimers and refund specifics. I see so many people in groups asking for a 'free' template to use. Equally lots of comments such as "I just took this one from this website's page."

While you may get lucky and not need to rely on these, I would suggest this is a pretty substantial risk to take for something that could potentially ruin your business. There is also a question over copyright. Is that fear-mongering? Depends on your attitude to risk, I think.

If you want to see an example of a simple sales page for our Perfect Toast course, please head to **GetThatCourseOnline.com/Toast** to see what I've put together.

Sales pages for corporate organisations

If you are creating your course exclusively to sell into corporate organisations, you may not need to have a sales page at all. It can depend on what you are selling — a course as a stand-alone product or as part of a bigger programme? Either way, you are unlikely to be encouraging people to sign up and pay immediately as you would for individuals. You're much more likely to see success through inviting them to get in touch for a discussion to establish their exact needs.

If you need to have something, somewhere, then your 'call to action' won't be a 'buy now' button as suggested in the pricing block, but a 'get in touch' button. Also, when you're selling into a corporate organisation, you are typically talking to the person buying, but not the person consuming your content. So how do you approach the copy for the sales page?

In this situation, I would suggest you first revisit some of the actions listed in Chapters Three, Four and Five, with your buying or commissioning target person as the focus of your attention. What's their biggest headache in relation to your subject matter? What's the one thing around this subject that they need individuals or teams in their organisation to get better at? How can you help them see your online course as the solution to that problem?

From there, you can take elements of a simple sales page structure and build to appeal to your target. I would approach it from the 'trusted advisor' angle — write it as though they have asked you how they can get this niggly issue off their To Do list.

For the specific blocks, I would keep the order of the first six blocks, but obviously rewrite them from the point of view of your buying or commissioning person. After that I would lose the final eight blocks and replace them with a simple call to action to get in touch to discuss how you could help.

> **Pro tip:** include somewhere in your copy anything specific you can provide in terms of how much money your course could save the organisation. It's relatively easy to provide a plausible figure here: think about an average salary for the people your course is aimed at e.g. junior managers.
>
> Work out what their hourly rate would be from that salary (working hours in a year), then multiply that number by the number of hours your course would save those junior managers in a typical week. Multiply that back up to a year and then you have a number.
>
> And of course, depending on the number of junior managers they have to attend the course, you can multiply it up again. This sort of information will catch the eye of any discerning corporate training or learning and development manager.

As a final note, if you are unsure about your writing ability, you might be tempted to keep going back and 'tweaking' your sales page. It is highly unlikely that after the third go around, you will be making any difference that will make a difference, unless something is broken (the link to pay isn't working for example). Force yourself to stop and say: 'Done is better than perfect.'

CHAPTER FOURTEEN KEY POINTS

- ★ Your sales page is important, but it is not the sum of your marketing. It is the 'convincer' for a connection that started elsewhere.
- ★ It shows your potential learner what they're expecting to find out and what they need to know.
- ★ For now, you can consider a sales page and a landing page to be the same thing.
- ★ Features are the tangible aspects of your course and the benefits are the intangible, emotional upside of taking your course.
- ★ A simple sales page has fourteen blocks that can be enhanced with appropriate imagery. There are fewer blocks needed for a sales page aimed at corporate contacts.
- ★ Ensure you have terms and conditions attached to an order page for your course.

ACTIONS TO GET THAT COURSE ONLINE

- [ ] Review the actions you were asked to complete at the end of Chapters Three, Four and Five. These will be the basis of your sales page.
- [ ] Start by loosely adding information into each block. Don't try to wordsmith as you go.
- [ ] Go back through the page to refine your copy (words) a maximum of three times. After this, unless something is broken, do not be tempted to do any more for now!

Get a handy PDF download of all the chapter summaries and actions at **GetThatCourseOnline.com/Resources**

15

How to prepare for blast off

CHAPTER FIFTEEN

T-minus ten – getting ready to launch

15

If you have spent any time researching online courses, then you will have certainly come across the concept of launching your course. You may even have been tempted by some of the 'names' in this space to sign up to their programmes — there are some very good ones out there too. My personal recommendation is Bushra Azhar.

But before we go down that path, it's worth having an overview of the assorted options open to you and things to consider before diving into a launch.

Launching (done well) can be a fantastic way of creating interest and sales. But you don't have to do it at all. You don't have to invest all the time and effort needed to launch well. You can simply make your course available and take it from there. Remember this is about what's right for you, right now.

Do you have your audience yet?

If you don't already have an audience of fans you are in regular communication with, you will need to consider an awareness-raising stage prior to any launch. This is designed to bring new people to your acquaintance to begin the process of getting to know, like and trust you. People have to know, like and trust you before they will buy.

Remember I talked in the previous chapter about how a sales page is the 'Convincer' coming after the Introduction and Nurturing stages? Your awareness-raising is at the Introduction end of this. You are trying to find people who are a) interested in your subject and b) like the way you talk about it. Ideally you want these people to actively tell you who they are.

The most common way of doing this is with something called a 'lead magnet.' There's a deeper explanation in Chapter Eighteen, but the essential elements are that you give away a valuable piece of content in return for (at minimum) someone's email address. You can charge for a lead magnet, but this is a more advanced strategy than we'll go into in this book. Remember 'value' is in the perception of the receiver.

Once you have someone's email address (ensuring you have followed all relevant legislation around data protection of course), you can start to go deeper with your introduction to you and your expertise. This is commonly done through a weekly email newsletter or similar.

It doesn't have to be complicated! Just a few paragraphs about you in relation to your expertise and perhaps a little nugget of wisdom, or piece of information to help them think more about the subject you have in common. If you are stuck for what to write, sign up to a few email newsletters from people you are drawn to and see what they do.

When we talk about launching, really this is another way of saying selling. That is the purpose of a course launch — to sell courses. The reason so many people put the time and effort in is two-fold: to take advantage of the hype that can surround a well-executed launch (sell more courses) and to keep score with others in their network ("I just had another seven-figure launch!"). Some are also addicted to the launch 'rush'.

No doubt it can be lucrative, but it can also be misleading. The numbers bandied around can be intoxicating and quite convincing to newbie creators. As with everything though, if it seems too good to be true...

Listen, I'm not going to tell you launching is a bad idea — far from it. I will talk you through the main things to be aware of in this chapter, so you can decide what you like the sound of and then potentially invest time and money in finding out more. An equal aim though, is to bring a little bit of realism to what's going on and why some of the numbers you might see advertised may be true but are often not the whole story. Caveat emptor!

By far the biggest thing to be aware of is that those talking about six and seven figure launches are 99.99% (estimated) certain to have access to an extensive list of subscribers (thousands at least) and/or have already sold to a good proportion of their list. While their launch activity will also add people to their list, if they didn't have a big fan-base to begin with, it's highly unlikely that they would see those sorts of launch figures.

If you don't have that sort of following yet, all is not lost, you can still launch. Just be a bit more realistic about what you could achieve and what that will cost. Remember all of those with the big lists also started out small and grew from there. I'm not about to tangent off into list-building activity in this book, but there is a bit of information in Chapter Eighteen. Start with 'Lead Magnet' and take it from there.

On Unicorns

You may have seen or heard the stories: "I got a six-figure launch with an email list of just fifty people and three of them were my pet goats!" Is it possible? Yes. It is likely? No. Can it be done without spending almost all of the alleged six-figures on marketing activity? Even less likely.

If this is your business model and you're perfectly happy with it, good for you. Personally, I like my marketing to be a little more easy with a little more profit.

Pre-selling your course

Pre-selling is a strategy where you release a very basic version of your course and ask people to pay you for helping to flesh out the details. Obviously, you need to have something for people to see in return for their money, but this doesn't have to be anything substantial at all.

The pre-sales strategy can sometimes be confused with beta-testing (explained shortly). If you are selling spaces on your course in return for help in creating the course, this is pre-sales, not beta testing.

If you already have an established audience who have bought from you, then you can use pre-sales quite effectively. Those people are already fans, so if you then ask them to help you create something new for a knock-down price, it's kind of a sure thing that you will get some take up.

Even better if you have already segmented your audience into those who have bought a lot from you (good indication of a super-fan), those who have only bought a little and those who haven't bought yet.

It's an attractive premise and borrows significantly from established product and manufacturing development methodology. It relies on the existence of a Minimum Viable Product (remember this from Chapter Six?). Each round of pre-selling raises more money from people who buy into not only helping to build the course but getting whatever the finished version will be for a great initial price.

But that is also where it can get a little too close to the shady end of the market for my liking. There are some who think pre-sales for online courses means selling something that doesn't exist at all yet. They use it as a way to test their idea, not a way to refine their basic course content.

Now evaluating your idea isn't necessarily a terrible thing but selling thin air with a promise that there'll be something produced eventually is not a strategic road I would advise you to go down. I've known good people fall into this trap and then for whatever reason not come up with the goods. The reputational risk (not to mention the refund bill) is not worth it.

I am not an advocate of pre-sales strategies for newbie course creators — especially if you don't yet have a big audience of fans. Does it show?!

Newbies don't have the experience to understand how to keep a course within a tight scope so it doesn't become too big or unwieldy for the price. There's also the risk that it becomes quite disjointed as different people have different demands of the content.

Without having understanding and experience of all the steps that go into creating a course before you use this strategy, there's another huge risk: you end up with a project that feels like a giant cape of wish-I'd-never-started-this-stupid-thing on your shoulders. And I don't want that for you.

I'm not going to say 'never' use this strategy, but I am very firmly saying 'not now.'

Beta testing

Unlike pre-selling, beta testing is not about course development but course refinement. This is about finding the flaws in what you've produced once you have built your course and feel like it's ready for the world.

Your beta testers are there specifically to spot errors, omissions, broken links, unclear instruction, unclear steps and to evaluate your assertions around how long or in-depth the course is.

Beta testing is often used to 'soft launch' a course. It's offered out — sometimes exclusively to a specific group such as your super-fans or trusted friends — either for free or at a heavy discount. The deal is that these people will review your course with a critical eye and supply you with constructive feedback to make it even better.

You can also ask your beta testers to supply you with a testimonial which will help with the social proof block on your sales page. Please note that feedback and testimonials are separate things. Feedback is a private conversation between you and your tester and you may or may not take on board their suggestions. Testimonials should contain persuasive praise only (see Chapter Eighteen for more), which will be used in your marketing such as on your sales page, in social media posts and elsewhere on your website.

If you have given someone free or heavily discounted access to your expert work, please do not be shy about pushing them for what you need. There are ways you can make this easy for them, but ultimately, they are receiving their end of the bargain so you deserve yours too.

Evergreen vs limited access

Broadly speaking, there are two options for you concerning your course's availability which may influence your decision about launching or not.

An **evergreen course** is one that is offered year-round, with no restriction on when you can sign up to it. Once it is launched initially, barring a complete rewrite/refilm, it relies on ongoing publicity to keep learners coming in.

There is a way around this if you want to have an evergreen course but also want to take advantage of having a big launch in a recurring way. This involves having only the basic course available year-round at full price, but then offering high perceived value bonuses and either discounts or favourable payment options at specified times, known as 'launch windows.'

A **limited access course** is one that is only available for learners to enrol at specific times of the year. There are several big 'names' in the online space that do this. They will gear up everything for a specific time of year to launch and have their 'cart open' (think online shopping cart). The launch window here will usually be a week — two at the outside.

Part of the reason these big names do this is because they are 'all' in the same network where they promote each other to their own lists, so they don't want to be launching at the same time. They promote each other using affiliate links, which means for every person they lead to sign up to their mate's course, they receive a percentage of the sale.

Hopefully you can see how this would contribute to the seven-figure launch stories you hear about? If you have just five people all promoting one thing to their list of 200,000, then that's a million people all hearing about the same course from someone they already know like and trust.

I know that lots of people will be on several of these lists, so there is cross-over of course, but the strategy is solid. And it works! More on this at the end of the next chapter where I cover increasing your chances of a big return on your launch.

Cynical me raises an eyebrow at the number of messages sent around the time of e.g. "Bob's" annual launch talking about "my very good friend Bob who's got a great offer for you". It's so obviously an affiliate relationship, that I tend to wonder if they would still be recommending their "very good friend Bob" if there was no financial incentive to do so... Anyway. Cynicism mode retracted.

A well-executed launch takes a lot of work over a relatively short space of time, so isn't something that appeals to everyone. The very big launches will usually have a team working on different aspects in the background and you may not have that type of support just yet.

In the next chapter I will talk you through the main stages of a launch. If you would rather concentrate on simply making your course available or just using it as a complementary offering to other things you provide in your business, then you might be tempted to skip it. I would recommend you read the chapter anyway, if only to see how you can use launch elements — without launching — to warm people up to buying your course.

CHAPTER FIFTEEN KEY POINTS

★ Launching can be a fantastic way to start your sales, but you don't have to do it at all if it's not right for you right now.

★ If you don't yet have an audience, consider how you might build and maintain a connection with people who would be interested in your course.

★ Pre-selling is not recommended as a strategy for new online course creators.

★ Beta-testing can give you valuable insight into any 'bugs' in your course functionality or content. It can also give you a useful source of social proof through testimonials.

★ Your course can be available as an evergreen product or only at specific times — your choice may impact your decision about launching.

ACTIONS TO GET THAT COURSE ONLINE

- [ ] Consider your audience — do you have easy access to them to publicise any launch activity you might do?
- [ ] If you need to build your audience, put together a Lead Magnet to attract them into your orbit, then communicate regularly with them to deepen the know, like and trust in you as an expert advisor.
- [ ] Decide if your course is going to be evergreen or with limited access.

Get a handy PDF download of all the chapter summaries and actions at **GetThatCourseOnline.com/Resources**

16

The secrets of a well-executed launch

CHAPTER SIXTEEN

Ready, set, launch!

16

A basic launch is actually a very simple thing: you talk about your course being available on a certain date (pre-launch), you make your course available on that date and encourage people to buy it (launch), you remind people when you are about to close enrolment (limited launch window — nudge cart close) or you periodically remind people that it's available (evergreen — nudge did you know).

Basic launch sequence:

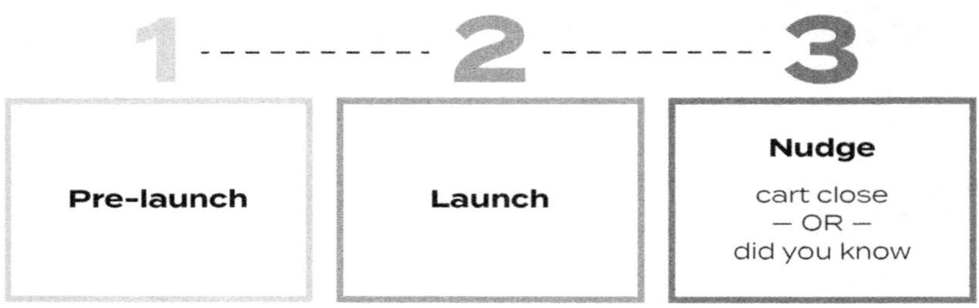

The structure of a basic launch does not deviate from the three stages above. It's the *methodology* employed during each of the stages that contains the magic. Just remember that the different options I'll explain shortly all work BUT you cannot launch without specifically making an offer — pitching — to your audience. Otherwise, it's like rocking up to an event, giving an unsolicited talk on your subject of expertise and hoping the organisers will somehow guess that you want to be paid for it!

Yes, there's no avoiding it. If you want to be paid for your course — you will have to ask people to consider paying for it. You will need to pitch. But don't worry — we will cover how to do that very soon.

One point to note is that launching as described in this chapter is really focussed on launching to individuals rather than corporate organisations. For more on the latter, see the end of this chapter.

Selling is about connection

If someone tries to pitch me immediately on making my acquaintance, that's a big fat 'no' from me — I suspect it's the same for you.

But I have no time for those who moan about being 'pitched at' after they have consumed a lot of high value free content. If someone wants to make me a paid offer to learn more after delivering some great content for free, I am happy to listen. Either it will be something I want to buy or it won't, but either way, I'm not going to accuse them of 'selling out' or trying to extort me or any other similar ridiculousness.

So next time you watch a free webinar, or take part in a free workshop, listen carefully to the pitch when it comes. Even if you know you are not interested in the paid product, use it as an opportunity to think about why that might be. You signed up in the first place for a reason, but clearly the end game for the instructor hasn't landed with you. Why might that be? What can you take from the experience to benefit your pitches?

If you don't see the link between the value offered and the price being asked, what is it that's contributing to that? How can you mitigate that with what you do?

Pre-launch options

A pre-launch is all about creating excitement and buzz about what's to come. There was a time when people weren't used to seeing a pitch for a product at the end of a pre-launch stage, so there was an element of surprise. I think most people these days are aware that a concentrated distribution of high value free content is probably going to contain a pitch at some point.

In a pre-launch, you are concentrating on the nurture phase of your relationship with your audience. You want them to recognise you as an expert, but also as someone who can help them attain something important to them. This could simply be more knowledge, but as we discussed back when choosing your topic in Chapter Five, it could also be helping them to overcome an obstacle or challenge.

The precise nature and content of your pre-launch will depend a little on your preferences, your audience and the nature of your main offer. The general premise is that you give people something of value in return for their attention and you create anticipation for the main offer.

You let them know about your pre-launch activity through any channels you have available: email, social media, your website etc. Remember your pre-launch is all about enticing people to want to see your pre-launch event, not your main course yet.

There are three core delivery mechanisms to consider: email, video and webinar. While you can stick to only using one type, the most successful launches will use at least two if not all three. There is also a recurring trend towards using a series of webinars in a 'Challenge' style of event, where there is a clear outcome to be achieved.

Using the Challenge method can also double-up as a lead magnet but be aware that the newer people are to your circle, the less likely they are to buy immediately. That's not to say people won't buy from you after one interaction such as a Challenge, but it is likely that most of your buyers will have known of you for a little while.

Knowing what to deliver in a pre-launch can sometimes cause a block for people — they just don't know what to talk about. This is understandable — you've spent time considering what the topic of your course should be to the exclusion of other ideas. It's time to go back to your original list of ideas we developed in Chapter Six — maybe there's something in your Possible or Overkill lists that might be suitable.

Here are some ideas for the type of content you could consider:

1. **Prequel:** think of this like a Foundation level. What do they need to know or understand prior to learning from your main offer? If we were considering our 'Perfect Toast' example of previous chapters, we might think a good Prequel for that course is something about understanding what snacks are and why we might choose to snack outside of mealtimes.

2. **Complementary:** this is something that will sit nicely alongside your main offer. You might position it as equal in value to know (but not necessarily equal in length to teach). Looking again at our 'Perfect Toast' course, this could be something like '*How to Make the Perfect Cuppa*' — tea and toast go very well together after all!

3 **Two Sides of the Triangle:** this is one of my favourites. I talk about what I call the Triangle of Training: people need to know the three tips of the Triangle — the What, the Why and the How — to learn a concept. In this pre-launch sequence, you give just enough information for people to understand What something specifically is and Why it's important, but the How to create it is your main offer. With 'Perfect Toast', this would mean talking about why making this snack is important, what needs to be in place for it to be perfect, but the how to do this is held back, because that's the bit they pay for — the online course.

4 **Taster:** this works well if you have clear steps to a desired outcome. You use your pre-launch to give people one or more of the steps in your main course, but only enough to whet their appetite and leave them wanting to 'complete the set' and buy your course. With 'Perfect Toast' we might deliver our Section Two (Preparation) lessons — when to have toast and bread selection.

Any of these could work for a single event, although some might be a little long. Most launch strategists will tell you to have more than one event (more than one email, video or webinar). There are a couple of reasons for this: a) it creates more buzz if you pre-launch over a few days or weeks — even up to a month. People have time to get invested in what you're showing them and they also have time to invite their friends along; b) you have additional time to embed yourself as a trusted advisor in their brain — the higher the level of know, like and trust, the higher the likelihood of buying.

If you're using a series of events, you want to create a sequence so that there is incentive to keep coming back for more. You do this through what's known as 'loops.' When you talk about your first event, you are opening a loop of new knowledge that your audience wants. During that event, you close the first loop of knowledge, but not before opening the second loop — which is what you discuss in the second event.

Knowledge loops:

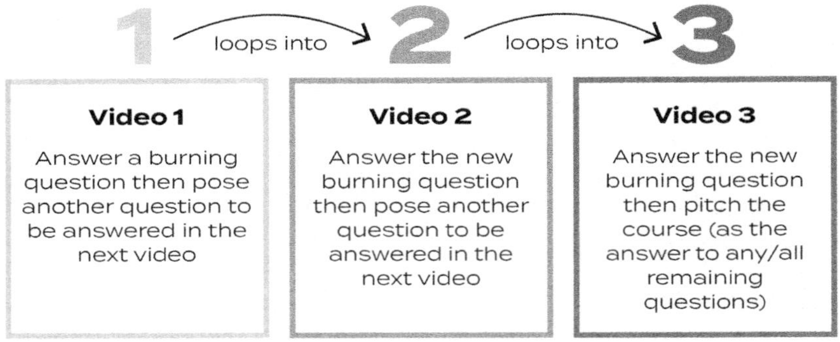

When you first use this technique, the loop needn't be any more complicated than: "Coming up tomorrow, I'm going to tell you all about...". Make it compelling by ensuring you talk about it in terms of WIIFM (Chapter Eight). In your final event, instead of looping to the next event, you move into talking about your online course — it's time to launch!

Launching

The time has come for you to make your course available for people to buy. Gulp! Be prepared for lots of 'what if' questions to suddenly crowd your head at this point. Just remember that if you have an audience of fans that you have really listened to, then you will sell online courses. The number you sell and over what period is subject to factors specific to your business, topic, knowledge, experience, name of your first pet... OK, maybe not that last one, but you get my drift.

Launching might be better defined as pitching, although that term is less appealing to people who are not traditionally in the sales professions. But pitching is what you are doing. Otherwise known as 'making an offer.' And really, that's all it is.

You are letting people know that you have something that would benefit them and letting them know how much money you want in exchange for it. Either they will want to buy it or they won't. If you have done everything you can up until this point, your pitch really doesn't need to be massively sophisticated.

Much like attitudes to the Sales Page though, people tend to put much more weight on to the importance of the pitch than it deserves. Of course, you don't want to come across like a pushy sales-sleaze, but most people don't believe that they can be themselves and still sell online courses.

There are some core principles to remember for your pitch, which I will talk about shortly, but please keep this as your main focus: you don't need a personality transplant to pitch successfully.

You don't need to suddenly turn into a shouty, brash person if that's not who you are. Of course, it helps if you can sound excited about your own product (if you're not at least a teensy bit excited, then it's time to rethink the course). But there are ways of communicating excitement that don't need you to suddenly be proficient in stand-up comedy!

A standard, basic pitch sequence looks a little like the following graphic. This can be used verbally, or more commonly with a visual aid such as a slide deck, using words or images or both:

Standard basic pitch sequence (e.g. on slides):

Let's go through each stage briefly — and remember you have all the information for this in the work you have already done in previous chapter actions.

Desired state: start by describing what life is like for someone who has achieved the goal your course is the solution for. What do they have, what can they do, all the things you can think of that tap into the reasons why they will buy your course (remember this from Chapter Five?). Ask your audience to imagine themselves in that picture.

Biggest frustrations of current state: bring them back to reality and where they are now by talking about all the blockers they face, the frustrations, the challenges, the obstacles you identified in Chapter Four. Really help them to feel the sense of distance between where they are now and what you had them imagining to begin with. The wider the gap, the greater the desire will be to close it.

Course introduction: now you've helped them become aware of the gap between where they are now and where they want to be, you can introduce the no-brainer solution to bridging that gap — your online course. You are just talking about the Title and Promise here, that you developed in Chapter Five. Our working example was:

'How To Make Perfect Toast: so that you can brighten your day at any time with this delicious snack, even if you currently burn your toast so badly the dog rejects it.'

Big benefits of the course: here we talk exclusively about the benefits of the course you identified in Chapter Fourteen. Talk about as many benefits as you have identified, spending time on each one to really drive home why this benefit is important (remember WIIFM).

Outline of course specifics and any bonuses with value: once you have outlined the big benefits, you can show the detail — the features. Try to fit it all on one slide to drive home the total value being received (assign a value to your course and all bonuses if you have them, plus a sum of the total value on offer).

Price being asked: on the same slide as previously (so they can see the total value on offer) you can now list the price you are asking — plus any payment options if available.

Perfect for, not for: list the positive characteristics of who your course is for and who it is not for. If you have any testimonials or case studies from past learners who fit the 'perfect for' characteristics, insert them here. Have some fun with this and remember to stack the aspirational characteristics in the 'perfect for' space!

Risk-free guarantee: show what you have written for this bit in your sales page block from Chapter Fourteen.

Repeat of full product offer and price with any urgency markers: repeat your product specifics slide with the price shown as well and then outline any urgency or scarcity that applies. Is the course only available until a certain date, or are you only accepting a certain number of people?

Above anything else, don't forget this one hugely, massively, crucially important thing:

GIVE THEM THE LINK TO BUY.

Yep. I have seen pitches where there is so much information being delivered and people are chomping at the bit to sign up and the instructor has forgotten to include the link for people to buy!

You want to show this link ideally around the time you introduce the price being asked, but you can leave it until the last slide if you want.

Nudging

You'll remember the graphic at the beginning of this chapter, which showed... ah heck, that's several pages ago, here it is again:

Basic launch sequence:

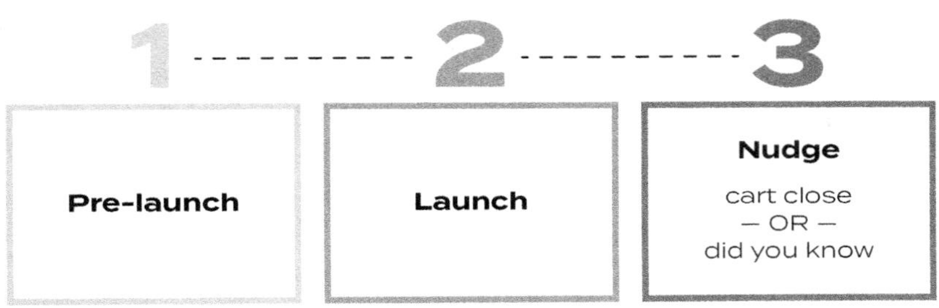

You can see that the nudge stage is split into two — largely because this depends on whether you are offering limited access to your course or having it available as an evergreen offer.

Regardless of your chosen route, you want to send your first nudge communication within 24 hours of launching. Hopefully you will at least have email addresses to send a nudge to (for example: "Did you hear the news? I've just launched 'How To Make Perfect Toast' and it's available right now through this link.").

If you are employing limited access, then you want to schedule more nudge communications in the run up to your 'cart close' (where you stop accepting new sales). As a rule, think about sending something 12, 6, 3 and 1 hour prior to closing. Yes, I know this can feel like you're 'bugging' people, but honestly the people who get bugged by it aren't going to buy anyway. As a strategy, it works. That's why it keeps getting used.

Anything you send via email should also be replicated across any social media channels or websites you have used in your pre-launch activity.

If you are intending to make your course evergreen, then your additional nudge communications will be more subtle. You want to make sure you mention the course in every email (part of your email signature) and every newsletter (a 'Did you know' section at the bottom or in a P.S. works well here). Also schedule periodic mentions of it in your social media.

Once in a while you might want to make a big push about it — perhaps if you have added new content or updated the course to account for an external change (software updates usually trigger this for technical courses). In this instance, you can use the pre-launch, launch, nudge sequence to encourage more people to sign up to the 'new improved' version.

How to power up your launch

There are a couple of options available to you for 'powering up' your launch — which is a semi-pretentious way of saying getting the attention of more people. The logic is that the more eyes you have on your launch, the more sales you will make.

This is true, but not exclusively so. What I mean is that as a rule, more attention will equal more sales, but there are some caveats in there. Those additional eyes still need to be part of your target audience and in the right place to buy.

While there are lots of options you could consider, I'm only going to introduce the two main ones for you, to avoid overwhelm — and remember you don't have to do either of these.

Affiliates: this is where you ask reputable contacts and associates to market your course to their contacts in return for a percentage of any sales made. An affiliate fee can be anything from 10–75% (so your affiliate is paid anything between 10–75% of the total course fee for bringing a learner in). Most affiliate deals I have seen fall somewhere between the 30–50% range.

You can get software that will automate a lot of this for you — if you are using a SaaS platform or decent plugin, they will have a way to do this. It is possible to do it manually, but it can be admin-intensive depending on the number of affiliates you have.

With a launch, you will ask your affiliates to bring people in at your pre-launch stage. You will need a way to track those people from pre-launch through to sale, so you can pay out your affiliate fees appropriately.

Affiliates can be a great additional marketing channel but be aware of the extra admin required to set them up and keep track of everything. Choose your affiliates wisely so that you know you are only getting good quality eyes on your activity.

Joint venture: we first came across this idea in Chapter Six when thinking about what information to include in our 'Perfect Toast' course. A joint venture is where you partner-up with someone who is producing something complementary to your course. In our example we considered someone who was producing something about making bread.

Ideally with a Joint Venture, you want to partner with someone who you trust will put in the same amount of work as you to make the launch a success. This is not as easy as it sounds. You need to agree who will do what; who will be the face of the launch for which bit; who will drive the pitch; what existing audience numbers (fans) you both bring to the table in the beginning; how you will collect and split the proceeds.

Unless you are starting a business together, one of you will probably collect the money into your own account. If it's not you, do you trust the other person to pay you in good time? Do you trust them to pay you if you have a disagreement?

There are lots more things to think about with a Joint Venture and I would urge you to consider having some kind of legal agreement drawn up — just in case.

Launching to corporate contacts

Launching as previously described might not be entirely appropriate if you are exclusively working with corporate contacts. They will be looking to buy your course on behalf of their organisation, for other people to consume.

You also may only be looking to include online courses as something that complements a programme of training or consulting provision. In this case a launch as described probably isn't appropriate either.

However, you can use elements of the previous advice in alerting your contacts to the existence of this new string to your bow. You will probably want to tell them about the course being available now. You might want to invite them to sample a taster of the course — you could make a single section available for free for example — so they can 'try before they buy.'

You can use some of the elements of the pitch sequence in your proposals. Here you explain the benefits of taking the course not only to the participants, but also the benefits to your contact of being able to get this thing off their to-do list. You did some of this work already in Chapter Fourteen when thinking about your sales page for corporate organisations.

CHAPTER SIXTEEN KEY POINTS

★ A basic launch consists of three stages: pre-launch, launch and nudge.

★ In a pre-launch you are looking to create a 'buzz' around your topic, so you can gain the attention of your audience.

★ In the launch stage, you are pitching your offer in a way that is authentic to you, following the standard pitch sequence and remembering to give them the link to buy!

★ The nature of the nudge stage is determined by whether you are offering your course as evergreen or limited access.

★ Affiliate schemes and joint ventures can bring more eyes to your launch activity, but also more admin to your launch.

★ Although you wouldn't use every element when launching to corporate contacts, there are still parts of a traditional launch you can use.

ACTIONS TO GET THAT COURSE ONLINE

☐ Decide on your pre-launch delivery method – will you use email, videos, webinars or a combination?

☐ Decide on your pre-launch topic, choosing from Prequel, Complementary, Two Sides of the Triangle or Taster.

☐ Put together your launch pitch sequence, making sure you are demonstrating the gap between where they are now to where they want to be.

☐ Decide your nudge stage plan and put together any assets (emails, social media posts) you need for that.

☐ If you are working with affiliates on a joint venture basis, ensure you automate as much as you can.

Get a handy PDF download of all the chapter summaries and actions at **GetThatCourseOnline.com/Resources**

17

How to make sure procrastination has nowhere to hide

CHAPTER SEVENTEEN

Bash those blockers – spot them, stop them

17

Through working on online course creation myself and helping lots of other course creators work their way through the process, I have compiled the top nine reasons people tend to get side-tracked from finishing their course. Here they are for you, so you can hopefully identify them early and use some of my suggestions to bash those blockers:

- Distractions
- Overwhelm
- Cramming
- Ignoring the medium
- Perfectionism
- Indecisiveness
- Conflicting advice
- No accountability
- No support

You'll notice that procrastination isn't one of the nine. This is because it's a symptom, not a cause. Deal with whichever of the nine is afflicting you and procrastination will have nowhere to hide!

Distractions

Otherwise known as 'sparkly objects'. When you're first learning about creating online courses, it's very easy to get sucked into the myriad of promises made by all sorts of online sources. These range from genuine to snake-oil and everything in between, so it's no wonder being distracted is a blocker to finishing your online course.

I've lost count of the number of 'secret ingredient' articles I've seen, where you 'just' need to sign your life away to get the magic 'one thing' that turns everything around. The reality, naturally, is much less sexy, but ultimately far more rewarding — you get your course finished and available for people to buy.

In addition to the sparkle and allure of silver bullets, you can also be easily distracted by all sorts of other things, particularly social media. Maybe you're someone who can focus intently and intensively until you're done, but my guess is that you've been distracted more than once by some kind of notification. We know we can switch them off, but what if...

Being distracted is fine, once we acknowledge that's what's happening and we can put some parameters on it. Maybe it's a twenty-minute window to check email that you allow yourself at the beginning, middle and end of the day; perhaps you have perfected the 'Pomodoro' technique (which is essentially using an egg-timer to measure out short, sharp bursts of activity); you might even switch off your phone altogether.

Of course, distractions don't just apply to trying to complete an online course, but if you're unsure of what you're doing and how to do it, then the distractions can get traction. Before you know it, the online course becomes something you were working on, once-upon-a-time. So here are some top tips for avoiding distractions while you're trying to get your course completed:

1. Pomodoro technique. As mentioned above, set a timer for a 20–45-minute window and challenge yourself to get as much done as possible during the intensive phase, with a proportional treat at the end of each burst.

2. Switch off the phone/email — or at least the notifications. Don't give yourself the excuse that it might be important. Unless you are genuinely expecting news of something time-critical, you don't have to be at someone else's beck and call, so set boundaries for when you will and won't allow yourself to be distracted.

3. Notice when you are best at specific activities and plan around that. For me, I work best with productive activity (doing things) in the mornings and planning activity (talking about doing things) in the afternoons, so that's how I plan my day. Sometimes I will work into the evening (particularly to get something finished), and sometimes, if the creativity's just not flowing, I'll take a random afternoon off (another benefit of an online business).

4. Focus on one thing at a time. It would be great if there really was one thing with online courses that made everything else easy, fade away, unnecessary, but there isn't. Find a good template or guide to follow for what you need to do and follow that, step by step. You've got this book, so that's covered at least!

5. Remind yourself why you're doing this. Whether you want more freedom and time for yourself and your family, additional income or something else, write it up, print it out and put it somewhere prominent in your workspace. When the distraction gremlins come calling, read and re-read your reasons until you feel strong enough to push them away. Just don't feed them after midnight, or y'know, get them wet... If that reference is lost on you, ask an older relative!

Overwhelm

Ah yes, that familiar feeling of so much information clamouring for our attention. Just how many articles, posts, webinars etc. are there on the 'most important thing' you need to know?

It can be doubly easy to experience overwhelm when trying to build an online course — possibly because your brain is likely to be telling you: "I'm only talking about what I know. Why is it so hard?!". We can forget that we're learning a new skill-set and that takes time to embed itself into our brains.

There's a new set of jargon to get our heads around, working out how to make the information exciting to learn, getting to grips with the technology needed, the hosting options, never mind all the sales and marketing needed. And that's even before you've worked out what topic you're going to focus on.

If you've experienced overwhelm, then you know what it looks like for you — most commonly it manifests as procrastination, so suddenly cleaning behind the fridge is of vital importance...

More seriously, it can also be something that feels more akin to a panic attack: you're not sure what's wrong, but something very definitely doesn't feel right; you might get clammy, hyperventilate or overreact to something you'd normally find inconsequential.

Should you find yourself in a situation of overwhelm with your online course creation, here are some tips for how to move past this blocker:

1. Take a deep breath and change your posture. Studies have shown that this simple act of simply 'sitting up and breathing' can do wonders for giving us a few seconds to reduce the intensity of what we are feeling in the moment.

2. Find a reliable resource to follow in a step-by-step style. Overwhelm often strikes when we're not sure of our current or best next steps and we can worry about putting in lots of work to find we've done something fundamentally wrong at the beginning. Once again, this book to the rescue.

3. EDPO is not just useful for working out your course content. Be realistic with what's Essential, Desirable, Possible and Overkill for what you're trying to achieve for this initial course. Don't give yourself too much work in the 'bells and whistles' department for what you want to offer your learners initially. I know this is one I can be guilty of.

4. Pick one (small) thing and concentrate only on getting that finished. When you're done with that, pick the next small thing and complete that. There's a reason students are taught to revise in bite-size chunks. Reduce your overwhelm by avoiding trying to multi-task. Studies have shown multi-tasking to be a myth — our brains are constantly swapping between tasks, rather than doing more than one thing at a time. Exhausting!

5. Ask yourself if you're really the best person to get everything on your list done. I understand that sometimes funds don't lend themselves to paying for many different services, but don't discount outsourcing a bit here and there to a good VA (virtual assistant) or finding someone with the skillset you need on one of the 'gig' websites such as Fiverr, People Per Hour or Upwork. Don't fall prey to the limiting belief that it's quicker to do it yourself than to explain to someone else how you want it done.

Cramming

"But Ginette," you say, "you've already given us what we need to avoid cramming in Chapter Six!" Yes, I have marvellous reader, well done, have a gold star. Unfortunately though, there will be many a newbie online course creator who only pays lip-service to the excellent information in that chapter and assumes they are already proficient at keeping their course content within scope. And so we talk about it again!

There are understandable reasons for cramming — we want to ensure our learners receive great value for money, we're used to delivering a 'complete package' when we talk about our subject face-to-face, we figure that more is definitely better than less and we're used to having complete control over what's covered, in what order and for how long.

Delivering in an online pre-recorded course requires a shift in mindset that can sometimes be tricky to master — it certainly took me a while to get my head around it when I was first learning to put together (successful) online courses. The key is always understanding the concept of learner-led control.

Your online learners have almost complete control over when they pick your course up and when they put it down. This has implications not only for the size of your individual lessons, but also the tricks and techniques you need to use to keep them engaged. And yet I still see so many creators attempting to convince people to buy a (e.g.) 20-hour course that gives them 'everything they need.'

This strategy is folly — online learners don't want to hear that something's going to take them longer than they can stay awake, let alone concentrate for. It's also highly unlikely that a single 20-hour course can truly deliver everything everyone taking it needs. The benefit just isn't specific enough.

Here's how you can avoid cramming, especially if you thought you'd got this one covered, but now realise the monster your course is turning into:

1. Break your face-to-face course components down into the smallest possible chunks that could be delivered in isolation. You are looking to have a list of individual lessons, which could be packaged together in different volumes to fulfil different needs.

2. Do you have the ability to chunk your material into Beginner, Intermediate and Advanced sections? Each one of these is potentially a separate course. All too often we assume people want

to know everything immediately. Learners don't want what you know now (although they want to know they can get there eventually). They want to know their first, second and possibly third step.

3 Could your individual course components be made to work in different contexts? For example, I used to teach how to set objectives in a course I ran on report writing. This individual component could apply to many different scenarios where objectives are useful to have. Consider if you actually have a mini-course within your main course that could be sold separately and as a bundle with other components of your original course.

4 Think about all of the additional information you could potentially talk about around your specialist subject(s). If you completed the exercise in Chapter Six with EDPO, you will be looking at your Possible and Overkill lists. Each new piece of information is a new lesson and possibly a 'bonus' resource you could offer. This works well if it's a small extension to what you've already delivered, such as a deeper-dive into a particular subject.

5 Go back and re-read Chapter Six of this book. Do it properly this time!

Ignoring the medium

You might expect me to argue that anything can be taught online. Well, it can't — at least not effectively — yet. My favourite example of this is learning to drive. You can only teach so much before someone needs to physically get in a vehicle and have that experience. Now it's not going to be long before virtual reality conquers that particular space as it has done for other methods of transport, but for now, it's not an accessible technology to most.

But this is less about online courses as a delivery tool in general and more about thinking around how you can translate experiential exercises into an online environment. It can be a blocker if you know the subject matter very well as a face-to face offering — especially if you've been expert in it for a number of years. You may fall into the trap of trying to fit a square peg into a round hole.

The ability to think of a different form of delivery is hard — particularly when that delivery needs to work for a learner in isolation. It also needs to be engaging and with just the right level of challenge — too easy or too hard (in perception or enaction) will result in it being skipped (unless you require some kind of formal assessment).

Imagine being asked to present your usual method of delivery of your expert subject, but there can be no audience interaction. Plus learners will be walking in and out at random points as well as probably doing something else such as checking their phones or listening to music.

That's effectively how you need to think about online delivery. So if at this point you're thinking, "Wow — why would anyone bother with online?", I understand! But really, it's a question of going back to basics and thinking about the best way of getting your training across so the learning is effective, motivating and engaging to continue.

1. Break it down. Only take a single chunk of information at a time and consider how best to just get that across. If you had to explain it to someone using pictures only, what would that look like?

2. Think carefully about your visual aids. Slides are great, as long as you have regular visual stimulation i.e. something on the screen should ideally be moving at least every 30 seconds. There is a balance to be had — too much information distracts from what you're saying; too little or too abstract (e.g. a pretty, but unrelated picture) and the minds will wander.

3. Make sure you are starting with your lesson learning objectives (Chapter Eight) — what's the reason for including this information? How could you help someone understand the point without spelling it out explicitly? Thinking about your topic in this way can stimulate your creativity in information transfer. Is there a relevant story or parable that will get the point across?

4. Are you using quizzes and tests effectively, or just lazily falling back on them as a way to train? Used well, they can complement what you've taught in your lesson, but I see them used far too often to 'prove' a lesson was effective. This latter method simply proves that the instructor couldn't be bothered to try to think about the learner experience. There's more in Chapter Ten.

5. Consider gamification principles in your course. You don't have to go all in on this (see what I did there?), but even just a simple 'well done, you're halfway' video in your course content can make a difference.

Perfectionism

That insistent desire to tweak just one more time, coupled with the fear of seeing the typo the very second you press 'publish' can add up to a whole lot of resistance to getting that online course finished! Perfectionism can also strike when we're unsure of our steps in creating our course — are we doing the right thing at the right time?

What I have also noticed is that this blocker has become something of a 'trendy fault' — there's even a Facebook group for recovering perfectionists. A little part of me wants to resist that though. Having ambitious standards to want something to be the best it can be isn't a terrible thing — it's only when we let it stop us from moving forward that it becomes a problem.

Which is the most important part of recognising and dealing with perfectionism — not letting it stop us from moving forward. In the case of online courses, this means letting go of something that we know could be better (e.g. video, content included, automation of offer etc.), in favour of getting something published.

This is partly because there's always going to be something that could be that little bit better. So accept that the very first version of anything you create is always going to be the worst version (even though it won't be bad). Therefore, getting it out of the way as quickly as possible, really is the sensible option.

1. Please go back and re-read Chapter Two of this book: The Online Course Maker's Mantra. You can't sell something that isn't finished. But you can definitely sell something that isn't perfect (people are doing it every minute of every day). Now repeat that mantra again and again until you believe it!

2. What's in your Minimum Viable Product? Write out the bare minimum you need to do to have someone be able to buy and consume your course and get ONE piece of wisdom from it. Plan out how much time every element beyond your MVP list is going to take — and how many extra sales you need to make to cover them off. It's surprising how much less important things become when we do this calculation. Chapter Six for the win.

3. Get good guidance. Make sure you have access to a good step by step guide, so that you don't get caught up wondering if you are doing the right thing at the right time. This helps with other blockers

too, but a good guide will teach you where you need to concentrate your most precious resource: your time. If only there was a book that could help...

4 Make it worth your while. Set up a proportionate reward for yourself, which you only get when you finish and publish. The reward must be desirable enough to be more important than getting that colour just right, or that bulleted list aligned perfectly.

5 Get some accountability. This is covered more wholly elsewhere but being answerable to others can sometimes be a good spur to avoiding perfectionism, because you need to get it done otherwise questions will be asked.

Indecisiveness

Another one that needs you to re-read Chapter Two and The Online Course Maker's Mantra. "I used to be indecisive, but now I'm not so sure" so goes the famous Tommy Cooper line (if you're too young to remember him, yeah, me too, honest). Joking apart, indecisiveness can be a real blocker to achievement with online courses.

It stems from being unsure about the 'best' way to proceed, which is really unhelpful as the best way is to actually proceed (i.e. do something rather than nothing). Whether that eventually proves to be a great decision or simply just a decision, there's nothing in online course creation that can't be changed at some point.

And yes, there's the worry about whether you'll be causing yourself more hassle down the line — I've been there and done that. Trust me — there's very little of what you first produce that you'll want to keep forever. The important thing is to keep taking those steps forward — no matter how small or large.

Sometimes we are concerned that the grass might be greener elsewhere. If we pick this platform, maybe the other will turn out to be better. If we choose this form of delivery, maybe learners will prefer something else. Perhaps the price is just that bit too high, or did I go too low?

There's always room to second-guess ourselves, but you will never really know until you commit to doing something and finding out. Here are some tips to help you on your way:

1 Get in a decisive mindset. We make decisions of minor consequence every day, and yet we can tell ourselves we are 'indecisive' in the face of all that evidence. How quickly did you get dressed today? Did someone else choose your clothes, or did you? When you last had that cuppa, who chose the timing and the strength of brew? See? You decision-maker you. Remembering and thinking about all the decisions you have made so far, will help you be in a mindset to make more decisions in the future.

2 Plan what you are going to do to help with decision-making. Do you work from research, or a gut reaction? Do you want to write a pros and cons list, or something more creative? The process of planning what you'll do to help you decide can make the deciding part that much easier.

3 Give yourself a decision time-scale. This might vary depending on the research you want to do but promise yourself that you will decide by a certain date and time and stick to that. You can even promise yourself a treat for it. You may have guessed I'm a fan of treats...

4 Find someone you trust to ask about the assorted options in front of you. It can help if they know what they're talking about, but it's not mandatory. Sometimes the simple act of talking through the options with another person helps you to make the decision yourself.

5 Own your decisions. This is about telling yourself that no matter what happens as a result of making a decision, it was the right one at the time (it will always be right because you've decided to do something). And even if it turns out to be a poor choice, you have still had that learning. Which we know is the important bit, right?

Conflicting advice

This blocker was one of the ones that annoyed me so much in the early days of my online course learning path — so much conflicting advice about what to do and how to do it. It took just that little bit too long for me to become a bit more cynical about what I was reading, but it was most definitely worth it in the end. The trouble was, it became a blocker because I initially didn't know who to believe (and I didn't want to believe that I was the same as everyone else!).

You see, the online course industry is relatively young and like any new emerging trend (think cryptocurrency) there are people around who are only in the business of pretending to be experts while actually looking to make a fast buck. I didn't realise this when I first started out making online courses, but my radar adjusted soon enough.

It was the amount of conflicting advice that really did it for me — until I realised that the people writing the articles and lead magnets were only looking at it from their own (and in some cases very narrow) point of view. The photographer who was suddenly the go-to-guy for course creation, simply because he'd created a successful photography course; the coders who were churning out 'do this one thing' type click bait because they knew people were desperate for the 'silver bullet' to a luxury laptop lifestyle.

I was lucky enough to encounter some like-minded souls pretty early on — people who were in the business to learn and help others avoid their own mistakes. With these connections and using my previous corporate nosey-parker (official term) skills, I compiled a massive list of best practice — where I could prove the efficacy of advice in online course creation. You can get this list at **GetThatCourseOnline.com/Resources**.

While there will always be conflicting opinions out there, there is also a lot more stability in what is being advised. It's easier now to find some solid words to follow. I have also got some tips for you below, that I would have loved prior to putting together my first online courses:

1. For short answers to simple questions, find at least three different sources that say the same thing. This isn't infallible, but if you can reasonably trust the individual sources, then the chances are the advice is solid. Getting the same thing from three different websites is usually pretty reliable.

2. Start from a position of best practice and then assess where you can flex. There's a lot packed into this tip but work with this bit first: if you are really the next Elon Musk or Jeff Bezos, you won't be reading this, you'll be out there doing your thing. So go with what 'everybody' is telling you to do and then work out later where you can do things differently for better results.

3. Choose to learn deeply from one person at a time, if they're teaching the same subject. So only go with (e.g.) one copywriting source, one Facebook ad source and one online course creation source. If you try

to mix and match, you'll find some conflict and that lets the blocker in. This is different to sourcing widely as in the first tip above; this is about who you trust to move forward with in your online course creation.

4 Trust your trust instincts. If someone (yes, even me) doesn't feel quite right for you, then they probably aren't. You will have enough new information to absorb, without also constantly second-guessing who you're getting it from. And just because someone doesn't feel right for you, it doesn't necessarily mean they're dodgy, it just means you're not feeling a connection.

5 Accept that there will always be exceptions to the rule, or people who found success with an opposing strategy. Often what you don't see is that they followed best practice first before finding where they could flex.

No accountability

I am fiercely independent — and in the case of putting together online courses, this was absolutely to my detriment! I didn't like the thought of being accountable to anyone — especially after leaving a corporate career for the freedom of freelancing. Why would I go back to having someone question what I was doing?

Of course, this was a ridiculous strategy — as you can tell from my hugely globally successful and critically acclaimed Networking Ninja online course... Nobody? Yep. Never published. Don't think I've even got the videos anymore. While I'm pretty good at getting things done, I'm also very much a last-minute dot com kinda gal.

As soon as I realised that the world didn't explode when I didn't get the online course finished, my productivity slowed considerably. What did it matter if I got this finished tonight, or tomorrow morning, or even the next day? No-one was queuing up in expectation of it coming (another hindsight mistake), so there was no-one to justify myself to.

This was ironically in stark contrast to how the rest of my business (at the time) was dealt with. While I was being supported by doing face-to-face work, there was no burning platform for the online stuff. Now that I'm mainly online, I'm less effective at chasing the face-to-face leads...

Two things made the biggest difference for me: recognising that my passion is with online and being involved with two accountability groups. I'd had the option before, but the groups available didn't feel right — and I wasn't in the right headspace to search for the right groups. If only I'd known then what I know now of course!

1 Not all groups are created equal. What works for me is that I am (still) in one group that is very small and we shared being on the same online programme together; the other group (no longer running) was larger and consisted of people who were also trainers but brought together originally by the group leader for a common purpose. I hear of other groups, some with a networking bias, some with a geographical bias, but I don't see the benefit to me because those things (physical networking and local contacts) are not fundamental to my business success.

2 Be honest and clear with where you are. If you don't feel that you can be honest, the group probably isn't right for you. The best accountability groups are ones where you can lay yourself metaphorically bare to get the best and most actionable advice for how to move forward.

3 Stick to your meeting schedule as much as possible. With my first group, we meet online weekly and have done since October 2017. We've missed maybe a dozen weeks in that time, usually because of a seasonal break or because someone is on holiday and can't get internet access. Sometimes it's tough, but the reward is more than worth it. We can ask each other pertinent and direct questions, because we have made a commitment to keep each other on track.

4 Recognise that it's OK to take more than you give sometimes and for others to do the same. As humans we feel a natural sense of reciprocity, so to take more than we receive can make us feel uncomfortable. A great accountability group recognises when one or more of its number needs a little extra boost.

5 Build relationships in the group by treating other members as you would your most loyal and valuable clients. If the group is right for you, the snowball effect can be extraordinary in helping you to achieve more than you could possibly achieve alone. I can testify to this one.

No support

When life is great, it's great isn't it? It's just that sometimes we could all do with a bit of a helping hand. And when you're in the middle of trying to work out how to put together an online course, having no support structure in place can be a real blocker to progress.

This isn't the sort of support that you might get from friends and family (equally important, just different). This is the sort of support that knows exactly where your head is at, knows the pain, frustration and unbelievable rollercoaster that online course creation can be.

Who else will know what you mean when you say you can't get the lighting right, or that the green screen fuzziness won't go away? Who else would be able to give you a morale boost on the days when you've lost a complete set of uploads, or celebrate with you when you get that first, tenth or hundredth sale?

Support — the right kind of support — is invaluable. Even if it's just having somewhere to go to ask a quick question, which could have taken a good half hour of Google-sifting. Not having to break your momentum too much by having a good support network saves you both time and money.

I am a huge fan of finding and sticking with groups (particularly online ones in places like Facebook) that you know you can rely on to be there, no matter what. Whether it's celebrating or commiserating and everything in between, I strongly recommend you find one that works for you, at least for the duration of your first online course build. If you choose to, come join my free Facebook group: **Facebook.com/Groups/TheGetThatGang**

For more focussed support — and support in online course creation specifically — sign up to the online course that complements this book at **GetThatCourseOnline.com/Course** and you'll get access to a dedicated Facebook group too.

Here are my top tips to bash this blocker:

1. It needs to be online course creation based. This might be the most obvious point in the world, but you don't want to waste time having to give superfluous context to your questions, comments, celebrations and rants.

2. What sort of welcome have you been given? The group might have a reputation as the best in the world, but your initial welcome will tell you everything you need to know about the overarching group culture.

3. Have a look at the sort of support and advice given to others. Is it pitched about right for you and where you are on your online course creation path? Or is it too simplistic or too technical? You might not be able to find this out until you join, but if it doesn't cost you anything, join, check it out and then leave if you don't get the right vibe.

4. Take a look at the group rules (if any). Are they lengthy and unwieldy? Are they so long they're housed off Facebook? This sort of group can tend to take itself far too seriously and is likely (in my experience) to have way too many self-appointed experts in it who often don't actually know as much as they make out...

5. How easy is it to get hold of the group owner? If they are often not around, or the group is mainly moderated by 'Admins' this may mean that you will get less support from people who know what they're doing and more from people who are learning at the same time as you. I've seen this work very well where there are trusted 'coaches' within the group, and also work very badly where the 'hosts' are so hands-off it's become a bit like the Wild West!

CHAPTER SEVENTEEN KEY POINTS

- ★ There are nine basic blockers that can get in the way of you completing your first (or any) online course.
- ★ Blockers can be bashed into submission in a number of ways.
- ★ Many blockers just need you to read this book and implement the recommended actions.

ACTIONS TO GET THAT COURSE ONLINE

- ☐ Be aware of the blockers so you can spot and stop them before they stop you finishing your course.
- ☐ Re-read this book and complete the various recommended actions.

Get a handy PDF download of all the chapter summaries and actions at **GetThatCourseOnline.com/Resources**

18

Sorting your sales page from your landing page and other helpful things

CHAPTER EIGHTEEN

Terminology

18

Every industry has its jargon and online course creation is no exception. There are even some terms that are used to mean one thing with one tool provider but used differently with others. You'd be forgiven for thinking it's a bit of a conspiracy. Here is a selection of terms that most commonly confuse new online course creators:

AFFILIATES

These are people (or companies) that will promote your course to their network in return for a percentage of the course price. The percentages can range from 10-75% with typical affiliate fees landing somewhere between 30-50%. The amount on offer is decided by the course instructor, although affiliates able to demonstrate larger audiences or conversions may set a minimum level for their involvement.

Experienced affiliates will usually expect you to provide an amount of marketing material for them to use (such as ads for their website, messaging for social media and emails), along with a solid system for tracking and pay outs. You can have a more informal arrangement though with a smaller group of business friends you know well.

AIDA

This stands for Awareness, Interest, Desire (or Decision) and Action. It's used to describe the standard route someone follows in the journey between seeing your course for the first time and eventually buying it. AIDA is a description of a Sales Funnel.

Awareness-raising activity is designed to let as many relevant people as possible know about your course. The idea is to find those people for whom your course is the solution they have been looking for. In launch terms (see Chapter Sixteen), this is where you would invite people to your pre-launch activity.

Awareness leads to Interest, which is where you start to filter out anyone for whom the interest is not strong enough. If they don't want to sign up to your pre-launch activity, this is a good sign the interest isn't strong enough.

Perhaps it's not the right time for them in terms of money or time available to complete the course. Ideally, you want to still capture these people if you can, so that you can nurture your connection with them. Then, when it is the right time for them, your course is the first thing they think of.

Once someone has shown interest in your course, your job is to move them to the state of Desire. This is what your pre-launch activity is designed to do. You want them to want your course, but this doesn't mean they are a guaranteed sale yet.

The sale is where you have moved someone to the state of Action — they have taken the action you want (buying your course) and have successfully completed your sales funnel.

BETA TEST

A technique used to flush out any obvious early mistakes or difficulties with your online course. You pick a small, relevant, group of people (Beta Testers) to offer your course to in return for feedback and testimonials. Covered more deeply in Chapter Fifteen.

CALL TO ACTION (CTA)

This is the bit where you ask someone to do something. It could be to sign up to your email list. For our purposes, it will be for them to enrol in your online course. It's astonishing how many people forget how important this bit is. Your CTA can literally just be a button that says 'Enrol', although psychology tells us it probably needs to be a bit more descriptive than that. Button wording is a whole topic in its own right, so be careful of this procrastination rabbit-hole.

CART OPEN/CART CLOSE

This is launching terminology (Chapter Sixteen), used to describe when you officially (and perhaps metaphorically) hit the big green 'Open' button and make your course available for people to buy (Cart Open) and then when you close it to any new enrolments (Cart Close). If your course is Evergreen, then you won't need a Cart Close, unless you are using a repeating launch cycle with time-limited bonuses.

CATEGORIES

See Sections.

CHAPTERS

See Sections.

COPY

This is the term for the words you use — typically in marketing messages, although in its broadest sense, any words you use connected to your business will be marketing! Your copy should have a style, tone and pitch that reflects your brand. If you choose to employ a professional copywriter, you will need to provide them with a good understanding of what your brand copy style is.

DRIP

Your entire online course can be made available to someone as soon as they make their payment. Or you could choose to only make certain bits available at certain times (usually so you can control what information your learners see and when they see it). If the latter is what you do, you have a 'drip fed' course, where you 'drip' out the information bit by bit and build up the learner's knowledge in a prescribed way.

EVERGREEN

Some courses are only available for enrolment at specific times of the year, but evergreen courses are available to start at any time. They may still have launch cycle that the course owner goes through, but the core course is permanently available.

FUNNEL

See Sales Funnel.

GAMIFICATION

This is where principles and elements of game-playing are used to increase engagement and motivation with an online course. It is mostly advanced online course design which I promise you don't need right now. If you follow the methodology outlined in this book, you have all you need to run an engaging online course until you are experienced enough to level up (it's impossible not to pun when talking about implementing gamification).

GREEN SCREEN

A type of backdrop for filming that makes it easy to superimpose a different background during editing, usually behind the speaker. Most of the time it literally is a screen that's green — it's a certain type of green colour that editing software can remove without compromising other colours. However, getting the green screen effect to look professional can be quite tricky if you're not experienced in video editing. Despite best efforts, there's usually something of a green 'halo' effect around you. Unless you have something to explain that is completely dependent on using green screen, it's not something you need right now.

KNOW, LIKE and TRUST

A pre-requisite for someone to want to buy your course. They need to feel that they know who you are, they like what they know and they trust that you can help them.

HARD LAUNCH

See Launch.

LANDING PAGE

Literally the page someone 'lands' on when they follow a link to your website or online course platform. A landing page doesn't have to be a Sales Page, but it is likely to be part of your Sales Funnel in some way.

LAUNCH

This is where you make your course available to buy. The precise moment that happens can be very quiet and almost insignificant through to a huge fanfare with lots of bells and whistles. I covered this extensively in Chapters Fifteen and Sixteen, but for the purposes of this chapter, there are three types of launch to be aware of:

Hard Launch: where the course is opened after extensive launch activity to gain as much attention from a target audience as possible. There is a very clear date and time at which the course becomes available.

Soft Launch: where the course is simply made available without much fanfare. Can also be where it is made available initially to a small group of Beta Testers (Chapter Fifteen), who will 'proof' the course before it is made available to the wider public.

Repeated Launch: where the core course is Evergreen, but the owner creates a launch cycle by offering additional bonuses for a limited time and runs a launch cycle around this. Many online 'names' use this technique just once annually to create buzz, excitement and an air of scarcity to their material (if you don't buy now, you have to wait a whole year for it to come around again).

LEAD MAGNET

A lead magnet is anything that your ideal audience would consider a valuable piece of information — valuable enough to give you their email address for, at least. Once you have their email address you can craft messages to help them get to Know, Like and Trust you more — which in turn makes them more likely to buy something from you when you make an offer.

For example, you might have created a PDF document that shows a list of the top ten things to remember with your subject; it could be an evergreen or live webinar training for something important connected to your subject; perhaps you have a 'cheat sheet' that helps them to remember specific bits of information.

A good lead magnet gives away enough information to show you're credible with your subject matter, without giving away so much information, your potential buyer doesn't feel the need to pay for anything more from you.

That said, all sorts of things can be used as lead magnets — including this book. In various chapters, you'll have seen me offer you additional resources for your online course creation. To receive these resources, you'll need to give me your email address through — and therefore this book and those resources become a lead magnet.

Having just said don't give away too much information, you might be confused as to why I'm calling this book a lead magnet! Especially as I promised from the start that you will get as much information as you need to create an online course — and I'm not kidding there — you don't need anything else if you are sufficiently self-motivated.

However, knowing and doing are different things. There are some people for whom this book will be all they need to Get That Course Online. For others, they may need a little more help. That's why this book is a Lead Magnet for my online course that follows the chapters here but provides a more visual learning experience.

The course is self-led with group back-up for questions. For anyone for whom this still isn't enough support, there's the opportunity to work with me, or anyone I have licensed to train my methodology, on an online one-to-one basis. I also offer an in-person online course creation Bootcamp experience.

Hopefully you can see how this book, while giving away 'everything', is also a Lead Magnet for the products I have available for people. For someone new to me and my expertise, it should act effectively to help them Know, Like and Trust me. If it doesn't, then they're not my ideal client.

Your Lead Magnet is designed to do one thing — get people into your Sales Funnel.

LECTURES

See Lessons.

LESSONS/LECTURES/TOPICS

These are the smaller chunks of information within your course — normally one chunk of information per video and one video per lesson. At least, this is how I'd like you to design your course.

In this book, the equivalent of lessons are the individual chapters — which, yes, can be confusing given how I also tell you that chapters are also sections... And just to confuse things even further, sometimes you will see sections being called lessons too!

As long as you remember that your big chunks (or groups) of information are sections and the mini chunks (or individual pieces) of information in each section are lessons, you shouldn't have too much trouble understanding this stuff.

MODULES

See Sections.

PLOSIVES

Without getting too technical (another procrastination rabbit-hole here), these are a group of sounds that you can make when speaking into a microphone. The way the sound comes across in a recording can be distorted and provide an unpleasant experience for the learner.

Typically, the letters in words that cause plosives are: b, d, g, k, p and t. You clearly can't avoid using these letters in the words you use! The way to minimise the effect of plosives is to use a 'pop' filter with your microphone. I talk about this in Chapter Eleven.

RENDER

This is the process of producing a video (or audio) file. Most editing software will need to 'render' what you have changed so that the final file that you will upload to your course can be produced.

REPEATED LAUNCH

See Launch.

SALES FUNNEL

A funnel is literally as simple as the first point at which someone is aware of you as a person who may have something of interest to them, through to the point where they sign up for your online course.

The marketing acronym for a Sales Funnel is AIDA as explained earlier and a sales funnel is commonly expressed pictorially using a literal funnel shape:

Traditional marketing funnel:

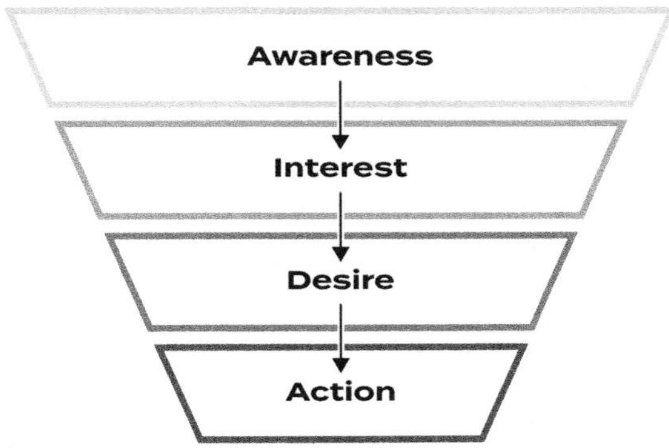

However, the funnel is not a brilliant metaphor as with a conventional funnel, everything that goes in the top, eventually comes out of the bottom. While it would be great to think that everyone you make aware of your course will become a buyer at some point, this is unrealistic. A better metaphor would be a bucket with holes in it, that gradually releases water, until what's left stays. You lose people from your bucket at various stages, until the only people left are the ones who buy your course.

That said, the word 'funnel' is commonly and widely understood to be the process by which you filter people through the process of AIDA, so we will stick with that.

At each stage of your funnel you will have what's known as 'conversion' rates. This is the percentage of people you can expect to move from one stage to the next. Your conversion rates are the things to concentrate on — how can you get more people to stay with you as they move through your funnel?

Procrastination rabbit-hole warning tough. For now, simply try to understand the numbers behind your marketing activity. Roughly how many people are making it from A to I to D to A? So if you double the number coming in at A, what does that mean for the number that reach the other A?

SALES PAGE/LANDING PAGE

Lots on this in Chapter Fourteen. Your sales page is designed to be the online page where people can find everything they need to understand what your course is and can do for them. It also provides a way to sign up and pay (if marketing to individuals — for corporate organisations, give them a CTA to get in touch with you).

Your sales page should not be the sum of your marketing efforts. If all you do is send people to your sales page and think that will do the job of convincing them to buy, please go through Chapter Fourteen with a fine toothcomb.

It's an important part of your marketing and your funnel, but it can't be the whole thing. Even if you are planning for a soft launch, your promotional activity needs to be more than 'visit this page' if you want to see success.

SCORM

Shareable Content Object Reference Material.

Obvious, right? Yeah.

SCORM is a compliance standard for e-learning, but it is not mandatory for all online courses. It's a technical specification for the videos produced that guarantees they will work on specific Learning Management Systems (LMS). They will also often have a level of 'in-video' interactivity built in, which requires them to be built (or authored) using specific software. Think Adobe Captivate or Articulate Storyline.

Unless you have a client that specifically requests a SCORM-compliant course, you don't need to worry about this. If you choose to only design SCORM-compliant courses, that's a whole other level of learning that isn't covered in this book. If you choose not to, your courses will still work on systems that also take SCORM-compliant courses, but you will need to have a conversation with your client about this.

The cost of SCORM-compliant authoring software is not massively prohibitive, but the LMS platforms to play the courses effectively can be prohibitive for smaller organisations. Clients that use SCORM compliance generally like it for the level of tracking it can provide in how learners are progressing through courses.

SCREENCAST

Another type of video you can include in your online course, this time referring to when you show a recording of what you are doing on screen. Most commonly used for things like IT subjects where you need to demonstrate what happens when different options are 'clicked' on or put in place.

SECTIONS/MODULES/CHAPTERS/CATEGORIES

These are the larger groupings of information inside your course curriculum — the biggest chunks of information, that in turn are split into individual lessons. You don't have to have sections in your course, but the larger the course, the more likely you are to need them.

SOFT LAUNCH

See Launch.

TALKING HEAD

This refers to a type of video you could include in your online course. It's where you are talking to the camera with few or no other items on screen, just you talking. For many people this can be a step too far for their first online course. Luckily there are other methods of recording your information, which you'll find in Chapter Eleven.

THUMBNAIL

This is the picture that shows on screen before a video is played. Most software will take a still image from somewhere inside your video. Sometimes this can work, but for a more professional look (and assuming your hosting solution allows it — most do), I would create an image to function as your thumbnail. Use the lesson title along with the course title and a nice image if you're stuck for inspiration here.

TOPICS

See Lessons.

WIIFM

The acronym for: 'What's In It For Me?' Helps us as course creators to remember that people will always evaluate what we put out for them to consume in terms of what they will get out of it. This is why we need to properly understand our target audience through listening to what they are saying. Once we understand what they want to achieve and most importantly why this is important to them, we can ensure our course and communication keeps their self-interest front and centre. A guaranteed attention-gainer!

Got a bit of jargon that you think should be included?

Email **jargon@getthatcourseonline.com** and I'll send you my interpretation and include it with credit into the next edition.

AUTHOR ACKNOWLEDGEMENTS

To those who have directly helped in the creation of this book, I am indebted to you for your precious time and sage advice. Particular thanks go to Anna Seabourne, Audrey Bodman, Christine Morrison, Emma Williams, Shelley Fishel, Stephanie Byrne. Also to Sam Pearce for her excellent book Stress-Free Self-Publishing.

A separate and special shout out for my ridiculously talented baby bro Phil Tessier for all the designery stuff like the cover, the layout, the graphical elements, the branding and more. If it looks visually pleasing, it's his fault.

Sharon "Firestarter" Gaskin: I will remember our conversation that started this all off forever. Without your guidance and support, that little acorn would probably have ended up in some squirrel's stash instead! Thank you for both the encouragement and the opportunities.

Anna and Stephanie "The Saggies": Thank you for indulging the endless months (OK, years) of me reporting in on 'The Book'. I hope I can repay your patience!

Emma and Kate "KeG": Apparently, there was a plot. There was definitely rum. Glad we're just as sane as each other.

Jazzy B: Mi familia. When we're terrorising the nursing home on our mobility scooters in our 90s, insanely high on Diet Coke, please remind me I wrote a book. And I'll remind you what you were saying when wotsit happened with thingummybob. Know what I mean?

To the 'rents and the steps: Thank you. That's probably not enough, so I expect some of this was your fault too. Love you.

Printed in Great Britain
by Amazon

24088080R00126